# 50 Shades of Stitches

## Mesh Knitting Patterns

with Step-by-Step Instructions

Copyright © 2020 by SCR Media Inc.

All rights reserved.

This book or any portion thereof cannot be reproduced or used in any manner whatsoever without the express written permission of the publisher.

Printed in the United States of America First Printing, 2020

ISBN **978-1-63227-3161**

SCR MEDIA Inc Box 7103

Delray Beach Fl 33482

561-909-6975

*If you like this book and found some benefit in reading it, I'd like to hear from you and hope that you could take some time to post a review on Amazon. Your feedback and support will help the author to greatly improve her writing craft for future projects and make this book even better. Just type this link into your web browser Getbook.at/Vol4 or scan QR code.*

# Contents

Introduction .................................................................................................3
Recommendations ......................................................................................5
Pattern 1 .....................................................................................................7
Pattern 2 .....................................................................................................9
Pattern 3 ...................................................................................................11
Pattern 4 ...................................................................................................14
Pattern 5 ...................................................................................................16
Pattern 6 ...................................................................................................19
Pattern 7 ...................................................................................................21
Pattern 8 ...................................................................................................23
Pattern 9 ...................................................................................................25
Pattern 10 .................................................................................................28
Pattern 11 .................................................................................................30
Pattern 12 .................................................................................................32
Pattern 13 .................................................................................................35
Pattern 14 .................................................................................................40
Pattern 15 .................................................................................................47
Pattern 16 .................................................................................................50
Pattern 17 .................................................................................................52
Pattern 18 .................................................................................................54
Pattern 19 .................................................................................................56
Pattern 20 .................................................................................................58
Pattern 21 .................................................................................................61
Pattern 22 .................................................................................................68
Pattern 23 .................................................................................................71
Pattern 24 .................................................................................................73

| | |
|---|---|
| Pattern 25 | 76 |
| Pattern 26 | 78 |
| Pattern 27 | 80 |
| Pattern 28 | 82 |
| Pattern 29 | 84 |
| Pattern 30 | 86 |
| Pattern 31 | 89 |
| Pattern 32 | 93 |
| Pattern 33 | 95 |
| Pattern 34 | 98 |
| Pattern 35 | 100 |
| Pattern 36 | 102 |
| Pattern 37 | 104 |
| Pattern 38 | 107 |
| Pattern 39 | 109 |
| Pattern 40 | 111 |
| Option 3 | 114 |
| Pattern 41 | 115 |
| Option 3 | 118 |
| Pattern 42 | 119 |
| Pattern 43 | 121 |
| Pattern 44 | 123 |
| Pattern 45 | 124 |
| Pattern 46 | 129 |
| Pattern 47 | 131 |
| Pattern 48 | 133 |
| Pattern 49 | 136 |
| Pattern 50 | 140 |
| About The Author | 144 |

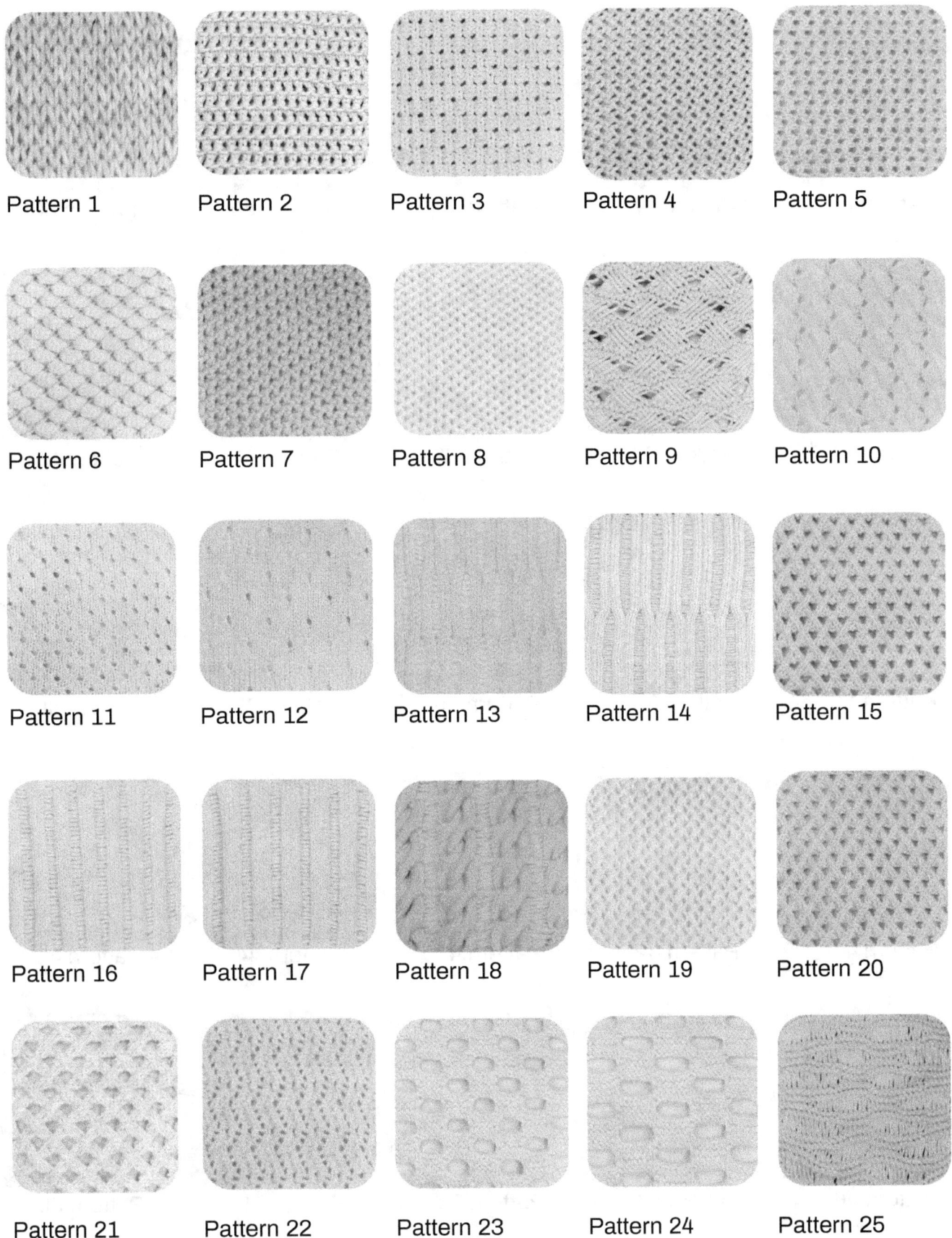

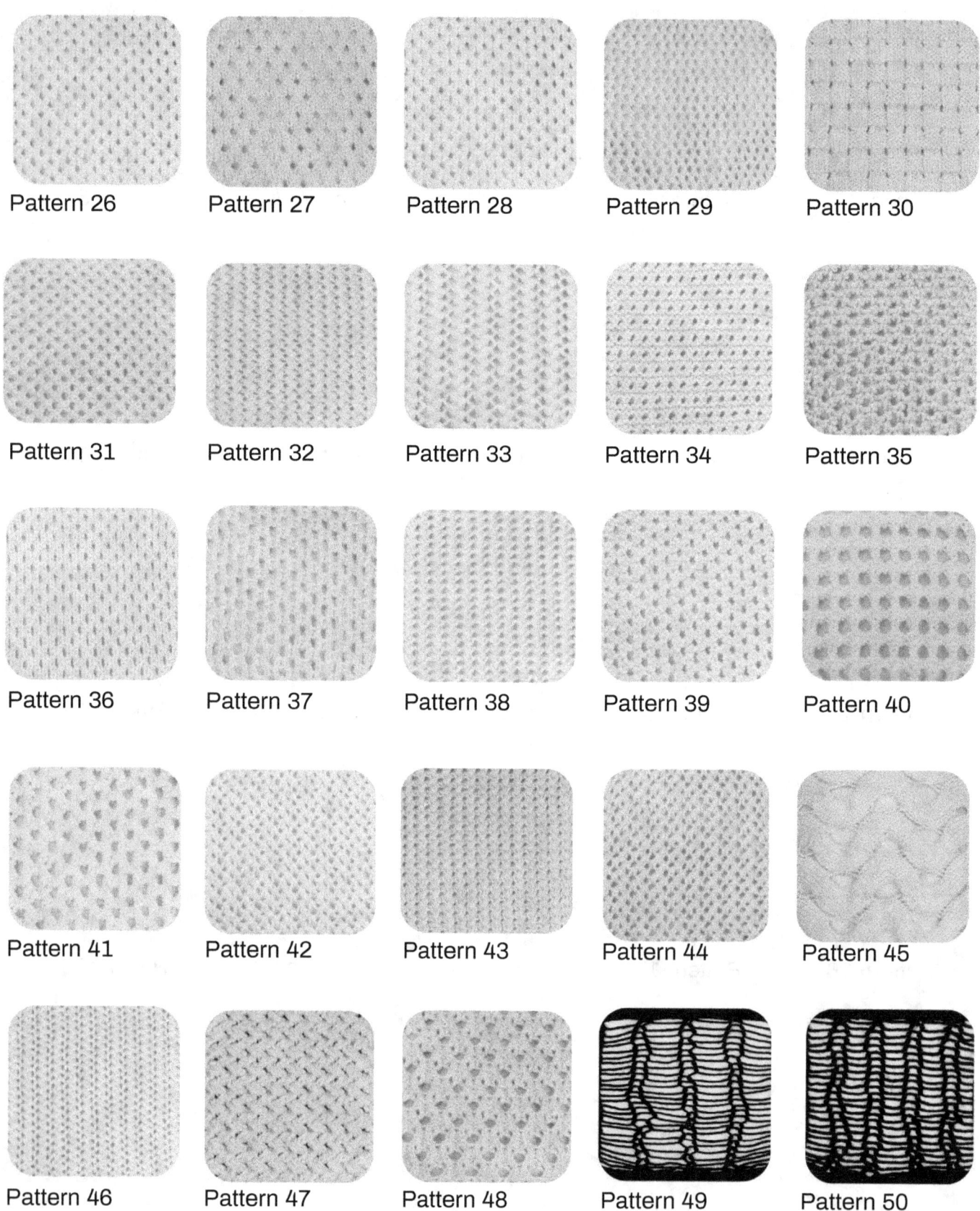

# Introduction

Not much we need to say about the knitting patterns offered in this book as they speak volumes for themselves. We would just like to make some comments that can improve the quality of your knitting, especially if you are a beginner, make your work more pleasant, and maybe, save you some time.

Although many patterns can be knitted without thinking much, many others require your full attention to avoid mistakes, especially those that contain multiple yarn overs. Practice shows that it is easy to misstep and to skip some yarn overs, especially at the end of the row before the edge stitch. It is not always obvious, but if a mistake is not corrected right away, it will distort the design of the pattern and lead to frustration and reknitting it; therefore, work all yarn overs mindfully, paying attention to each of them.

In the description of each pattern, we indicate how yarn overs should be worked: forward (i.e., from yourself) or backward (i.e., to yourself). If yarn overs are done incorrectly, it can also distort the design of the pattern; therefore, follow our instruction.

Slipped stitches are one more element of knitting frequently used in this book. As stitches can be slipped two ways, either knitwise or purlwise, we indicate which way a stitch should be slipped. Follow our instructions, as incorrectly slipped stitches, can affect the evenness of a pattern or distort the design.

Textile knots that used for connecting the ends of yarn can be too noticeable, especially in mesh patterns. If you need to make knots, do them at the edge stitches, at the beginning of a row or the end. This way, the knots can be hidden in the seams, making your work flawless. Another way to avoid noticeable knots is to connect two ends of yarn using a sewing needle: simply insert one end of the yarn inside the other one. This method works well, especially for thin yarns.

The quality of knitting always reflects on the quality of knits. It's especially obvious in stockinet stitches. And although knitting stockinet stitches is easy, somehow, at the same time, it is also difficult, as knitting them professionally well requires certain skills, accuracy, and a lot of practice.

To receive even stockinet stitches, focus your attention on the process of knitting, as each stitch must come out the same size. The tension of the working yarn is another important factor: the yarn must be tightly strained, and the distance between the working yarn and the tip of the right needle must always be the same.

Using regular needles instead of circular ones for knitting stockinet stitches also improves their quality. Somehow regular straight needles help to control the evenness of stitches. Stockinet stitches also look more even if they are knitted on thin needles, and the thinner, the better.

For stockinet stitches, it is also essential to use new yarn. Of new yarn, they come out more even than of previously used one—the difference is significant.

Lastly, if a pattern does not require a specific way of knitting, through the front legs or the back legs, consider trying both ways before deciding which one to use. In many patterns, stockinet stitches come out tighter, and therefore better, when they are knitted through the back legs, i.e., the second way of knitting stitches, which affects the tightness of knits and improves their quality. Stockinet stitches that are knitted through the front legs, i.e., conventionally, usually come out softer and, somehow, more even than those that are knitted through the back legs, which also improves the quality of certain patterns, especially openwork ones; therefore, try both ways.

For new ideas, consider knitting nets or other mesh patterns using larger needles than recommended for your yarn. Some patterns can come out better than they would be otherwise, and even, surprisingly, completely different.

As different or similar mesh knitting patterns can complement each other, consider combining various patterns in one design, thus creating an unusual collage of fresh ideas for stylish knits.

—**Marina Molo**

# Recommendations

**Knitting through the front leg:** Knit through the front leg, inserting the right needle through the stitch from left to right, purl as follows: with the working yarn in front of the stitch, insert the right needle through the stitch from back to front and wrap the working yarn forward (from yourself) around the tip of the right needle, then pull the working yarn with the right needle through the stitch. **Note:** The purl stitch that is worked this way sets up the knit stitch to be knitted through the front leg. This method of knitting is the most popular and known as conventional.

**Knitting through the back leg:** Knit through the back leg, inserting the right needle through the stitch from front to back, purl as follows: with the working yarn in front of the stitch, insert the right needle through the stitch from back to front, then move the working yarn under the right needle and pull it with the needle through the stitch. **Note:** The purl stitch that is worked this way sets up the knit stitch to be knitted through the back leg.

## How to Work the Edge Stitches

**The first way:** Slip the first edge stitch; purl the last edge stitch as if to purl in knitting through back leg as follows: with the working yarn in front of the stitch, insert the right needle through the stitch from back to front, then move the working yarn under the right needle and pull it with the needle through the stitch. **Note:** Regardless of the method of knitting, through the front legs or the back legs, purl the last edge stitch as if to purl in knitting through the back leg, as this way of working the last edge stitch creates more tight and even edges.

**The second way:** Knit both the first edge stitch and the last one through the front legs (or, depending on the pattern, through the back legs). **Note:** This way of working the edge stitches is used in patterns in which otherwise the left edge comes out loose and slightly stretchy. This way of working the edge stitches creates even edges on both sides.

## How to Do Yarn Over

Unless indicated otherwise, when knit stitch follows yarn over, the working yarn goes from the front of the needle towards the back. In this case, the description reads, "yarn over forward." When purl stitch follows yarn over, the working yarn goes from behind the needle towards the front. In this case, the description reads, "yarn over backward."

## How to Bind off Stitches

**The first method:** After the last row, turn your work over, to the Back Side; slip all stitches from the left needle to the right one, as a result, the working yarn is at the end of the row; turn your work over, to the Front Side; slip 2 stitches from the left needle to the right one, then insert the left needle through the 1st slipped stitch from left to right and pass it over the 2nd one (now there is 1 stitch on the right needle), *slip 1 stitch from the left needle to the right one, insert the left needle through the 1st stitch on the right needle, from left to right, and pass it over the 2nd one (now there is 1 stitch on the right needle)* repeat from * to * until the end of the row.

**Note:** This method is appropriate for binding off frequently intersected stitches and patterns that do not require an additional trimming, as this way of binding off creates a tight chain of small stitches that look already finished. For patterns that do require trimming, knit the last row and bind off loosely, using larger needles than the working ones.

**The second method:** Slip the edge stitch onto the right needle, knit the next 1, then insert the left needle through the slipped edge stitch from left to right and pass it over the knitted stitch (now there is 1 stitch on the right needle), *knit the next 1, then insert the left needle through the 1st stitch on the right needle from left to right and pass it over the knitted one (now there is 1 stitch on the right needle)* repeat from * to * until the end of the row.

**How to Count Rows**

Count the edge stitches, instead of rows, as counting the actual rows, especially in complicated patterns, can be difficult, or impossible. Each edge stitch is equal to 2 rows. Count the chain of the edge stitches as follows: 2, 4, 6, 8, 10, etc. It's fast and easy.

# Pattern 1

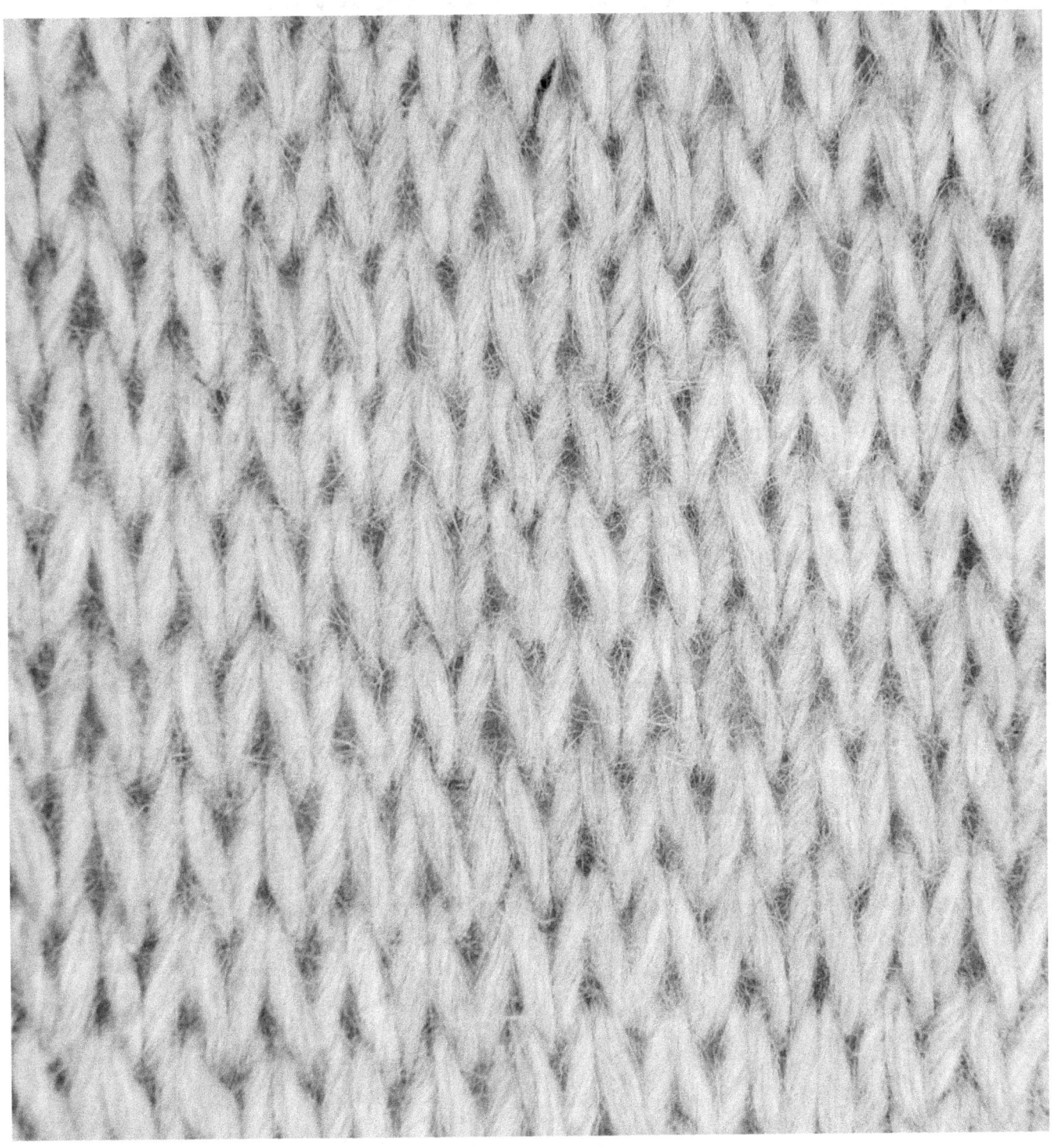

Cast on any number of stitches. Repeat rows: 3-4. **The edge stitches are not included in the description below and must be added. Slip the first edge stitch, purl the last one.**

**Knit through the back leg, purl as follows:** with the working yarn in front of the stitch, insert the right needle through the stitch from back to front, move the working yarn under the right needle and pull it with the needle through the stitch. The purl stitch that is worked this way sets up the knit stitch to be knitted through the back leg. **Use a bulky yarn.**

# Description:

**Row 1 (set up row):** *Yarn over forward (i.e., from yourself), knit 1* repeat from * to * until the end of the row before the edge stitch, yarn over forward.

**Row 2 (set up row):** Purl all the stitches.

**Row 3:** Knit all the stitches.

**Row 4:** Purl all the stitches.

**Repeat rows 3-4 until the desired length. Note: Knit 3 times less rows than required, as the length of this pattern increases 3 times as a result of sliding down the former yarn overs at the last row. Knit a sample first.**

**The last row (Front Side): Slip each former yarn over made in the first row off the left needle and leave it as is, then bind off the rest of the knit stitches.**

**Work this last row as follows:** Slip the edge stitch onto the right needle, slip the next 1 off the left needle and leave it as is (the former yarn over made in the 1st row), knit the next 1, then insert the left needle through the slipped stitch on the right needle, from left to right, and pass it over the knitted stitch, *now there is 1 stitch on the right needle, slip the next 1 off the left needle and leave it as is (the former yarn over made in the 1st row), knit the next 1, then insert the left needle through the 1st stitch on the right needle, from left to right, and pass it over the 2nd one* repeat from * to * until the end of the row before the edge stitch, slip the last 1 (the former yarn over made in the 1st row) and leave it as is.

**Slide down all the former yarn overs, from top to bottom, until the 1st row. As a result, the stitches become elongated, and the length of this pattern increases 3 times.**

# Pattern 2

Cast on a multiple of 2, plus 2 edge stitches. Two-stitch repeat. Repeat rows: 1-8.

**The edge stitches are not included in the description below and must be added. Knit the first edge stitch through the front leg; knit the last edge stitch through the front leg.**

**Knit through the front leg, purl as follows:** with the working yarn in front of the stitch, insert the right needle through the stitch from back to front, wrap the working yarn forward (i.e., from yourself) around the tip of the right needle, then pull the working yarn with the right needle through the stitch. The purl stitch that is worked this way sets up the knit stitch to be knitted through the front leg.

# Description:

**Row 1:** *Purl 2 together * repeat from * to * until the end of the row.

**Row 2:** *Purl 1, yarn over **backward** (i.e., to yourself)* repeat from * to * until the end of the row.

**Row 3:** *Knit 1 through the back leg (yarn over of the previous row), knit 1 through the front leg* repeat from * to * until the end of the row.

**Row 4:** Purl all the stitches.

**Row 5:** *Purl 2 together* repeat from * to * until the end of the row.

**Row 6:** *Yarn over **backward**, purl 1* repeat from * to * until the end of the row.

**Row 7:** *Knit 1 through the front leg, knit 1 through the back leg (yarn over of the previous row)* repeat from * to * until the end of the row.

**Row 8:** Purl all the stitches.

**Repeat rows:** 1-8.

**Bind off after the last row 8 as follows:** Slip the edge stitch onto the right needle, knit the next 1 through the front leg, then insert the left needle through the slipped edge stitch, from left to right, and pass it over the knitted stitch, *now there is 1 stitch on the right needle, knit the next 1 through the front leg (now there are 2 stitches on the right needle), insert the left needle through the 1st stitch on the right needle, from left to right, and pass it over the 2nd one* repeat from * to * until the end of the row.

# Pattern 3

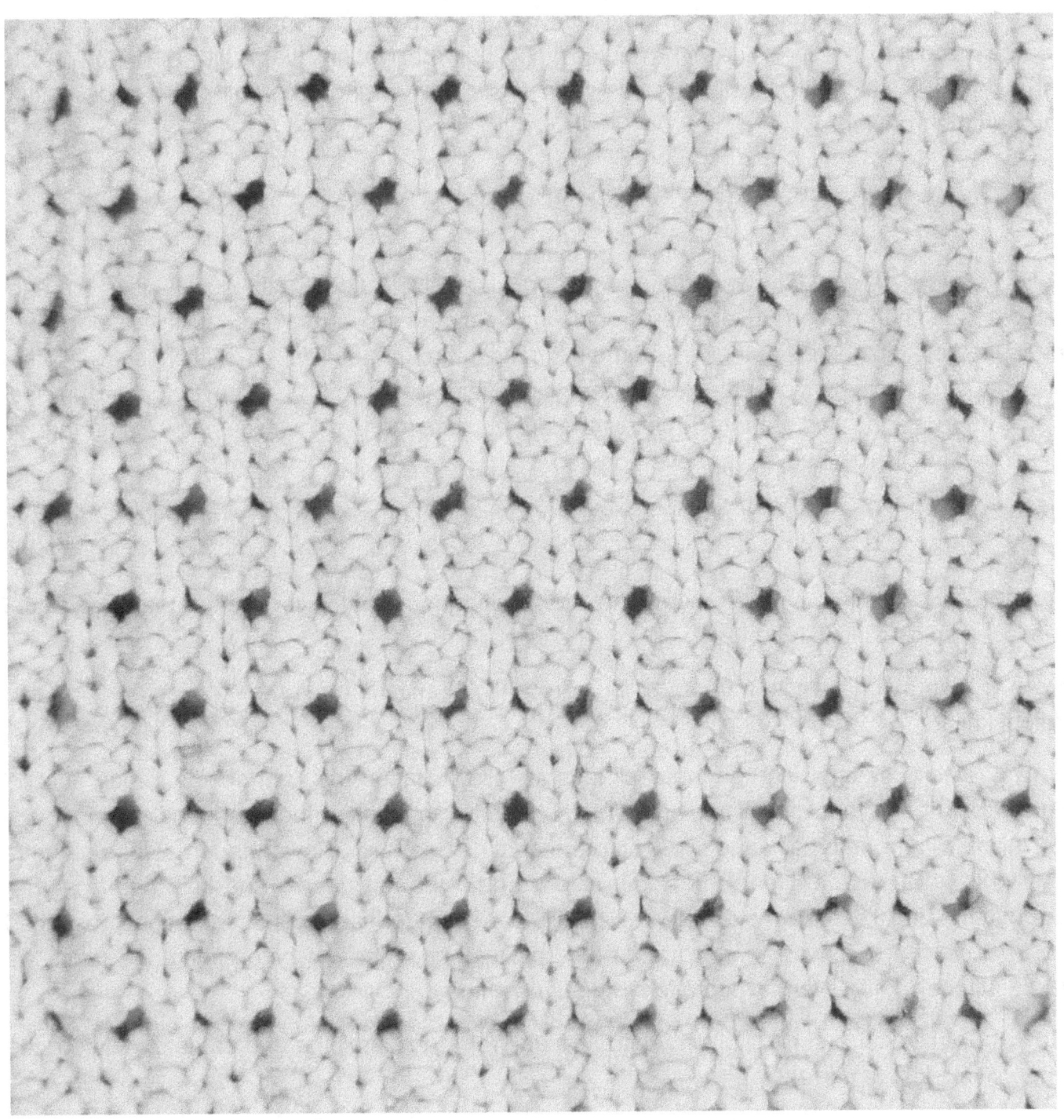

Cast on a multiple of 4, plus 1, and 2 edge stitches. Four-stitch repeat. Repeat rows: 1-8. **The edge stitches are not included in the description below and must be added. Slip the first edge stitch; purl the last one as in knitting through the back leg as follows:** with the working yarn in front of the stitch, insert the right needle through the stitch from back to front, move the working yarn under the right needle and pull it with the needle through the stitch.

**Knit through the front leg, purl as follows:** with the working yarn in front of the stitch, insert the right needle through the stitch from back to front, wrap the working yarn forward (i.e., from yourself) around the tip of the right needle, then pull the working yarn with the right needle through the stitch. The purl stitch that is worked this way sets up the knit stitch to be knitted through the front leg.

# Description:

**Row 1:** Knit 1, yarn over forward (i.e., from yourself), *knit 3 together as follows: insert the right needle through the 2$^{nd}$ and 1$^{st}$ stitches, from left to right, and slip both 2 stitches knitwise onto the right needle, knit the next 1, then insert the left needle through the slipped 2 stitches, from left to the right, and pass them over the knitted one, yarn over forward, knit 1, yarn over forward* repeat from * to * until the end of the row before the edge stitch, the last 4 stitches, knit 3 together as described in this row above, yarn over forward, knit 1.

**Row 2:** Knit 2, purl 1, *knit 3, purl 1* repeat from * to * until the end of the row before the edge stitch, knit 2.

**Row 3:** Purl 2, *knit 1, purl 3* repeat from * to * until the end of the row before the edge stitch, the last 3 stitches, knit 1, purl 2.

**Row 4:** Knit 2, purl 1, *knit 3, purl 1 * repeat from * to * until the end of the row before the edge stitch, knit 2.

**Row 5:** Knit 2 together through the back legs as follows: insert the right needle through the 1$^{st}$ stitch from front to back and slip it onto the right needle, then insert the right needle through the 2$^{nd}$ stitch from front to back and slip it onto the right needle, thus moving the front legs of these 2 stitches to the back, then return both stitches onto the left needle and knit them together through the back legs, yarn over forward, *knit 1, yarn over forward, knit 3 together as described in row 1, yarn over forward* repeat from * to * until the end of the row before the edge stitch, the last 3 stitches, knit 1, yarn over forward, knit 2 together.

**Row 6:** Purl 1, knit 2, *knit 1, purl 1, knit 2* repeat from * to * until the end of the row before the edge stitch, knit 1, purl 1.

**Row 7:** Knit 1, purl 1, *purl 2, knit 1, purl 1* repeat from * to * until the end of the row before the edge stitch, the last 3 stitches, purl 2, knit 1.

**Row 8:** Purl 1, knit 2, *knit 1, purl 1, knit 2* repeat from * to * until the end of the row before the edge stitch, knit 1, purl 1.

**Repeat rows:** 1-8.

**Bind off after the last row 8 as follows:** Slip the edge stitch onto the right needle, knit the next 1, then insert the left needle through the slipped edge stitch, from left to right, and pass it over the knitted stitch, *now there is 1 stitch on the right needle, knit the next 1 (now there are 2 stitches on the right needle), insert the left needle through the 1st stitch on the right needle, from left to right, and pass it over the 2nd one* repeat from * to * until the end of the row.

# Pattern 4

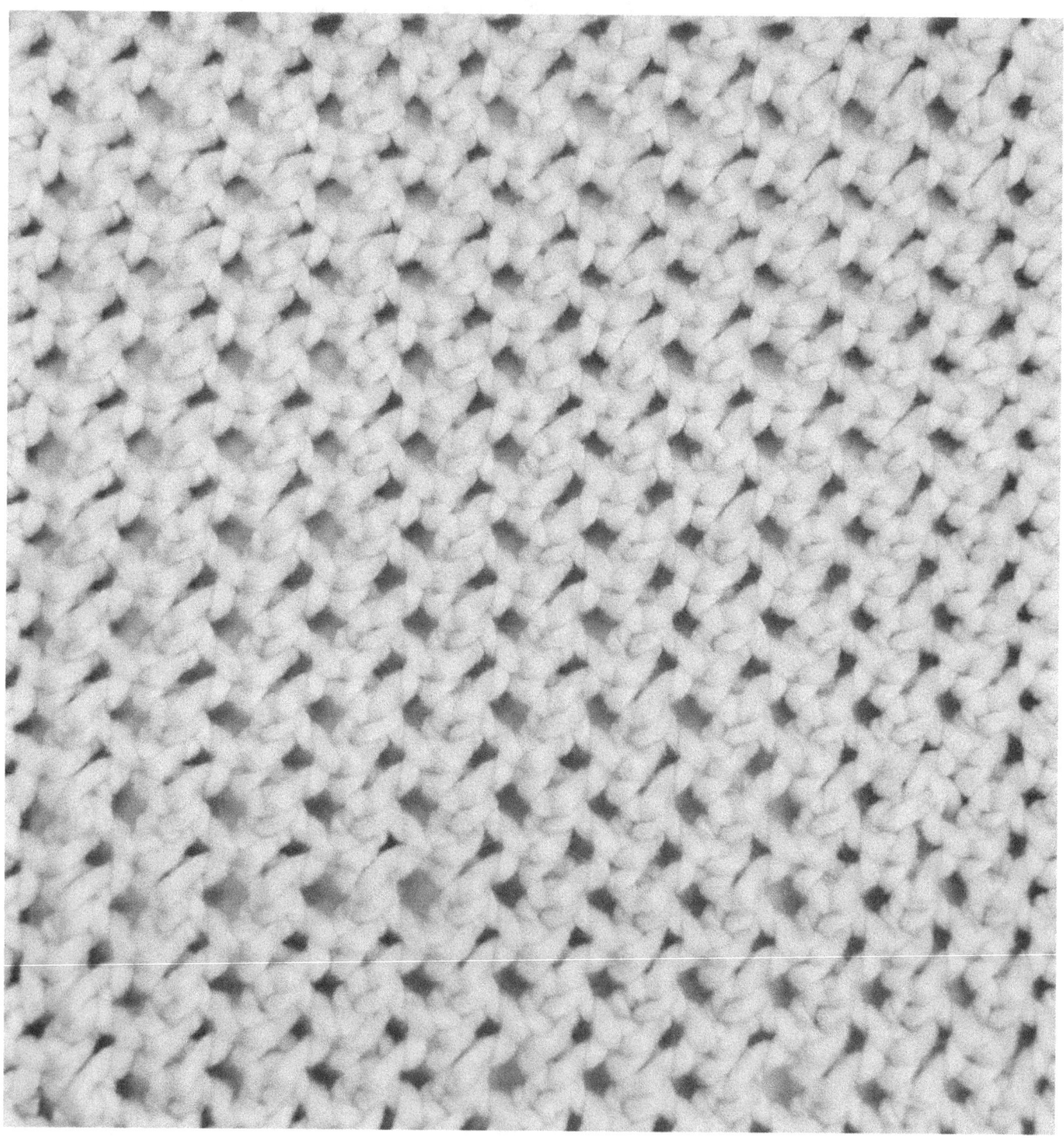

Cast on a multiple of 2, plus 2 edge stitches. Two-stitch repeat. Repeat rows: 1-4. **The edge stitches are not included in the description below and must be added. Slip the first edge**

**stitch; purl the last one as in knitting through the back leg as follows:** with the working yarn in front of the stitch, insert the right needle through the stitch from back to front, move the working yarn under the right needle and pull it with the needle through the stitch. **Knit through the front legs. Needles: U.S. no. 10 (5.75 mm). Use a bulky yarn.**

# Description:

**Row 1 (Back Side):** *Yarn over forward (i.e., from yourself), knit 2 together through the front legs* repeat from * to * until the end of the row.

**Row 2 (Front Side):** Knit all the stitches through the front legs.

**Row 3 (Back Side):** *Knit 2 together as follows: Slip the 1st stitch through the front leg onto the right needle, knit the 2nd stitch through the front leg, then insert the left needle through the slipped stitch, from left to right, and pass it over the knitted stitch, yarn over forward* repeat from * to * until the end of the row.

**Row 4 (Front Side):** Knit all the stitches through the front legs.

**Repeat rows:** 1-4.

**Bind off in the last row 4 as follows:** Slip the edge stitch onto the right needle, knit the next 1 through the front leg, insert the left needle through the slipped edge stitch, from left to right, and pass it over the knitted stitch, *now there is 1 stitch on the right needle, knit the next 1 through the front leg (now there are 2 stitches on the right needle), insert the left needle through the 1st stitch on the right needle, from left to right, and pass it over the 2nd one* repeat from * to * until the end of the row.

# Pattern 5

## Reversible
## Option 1

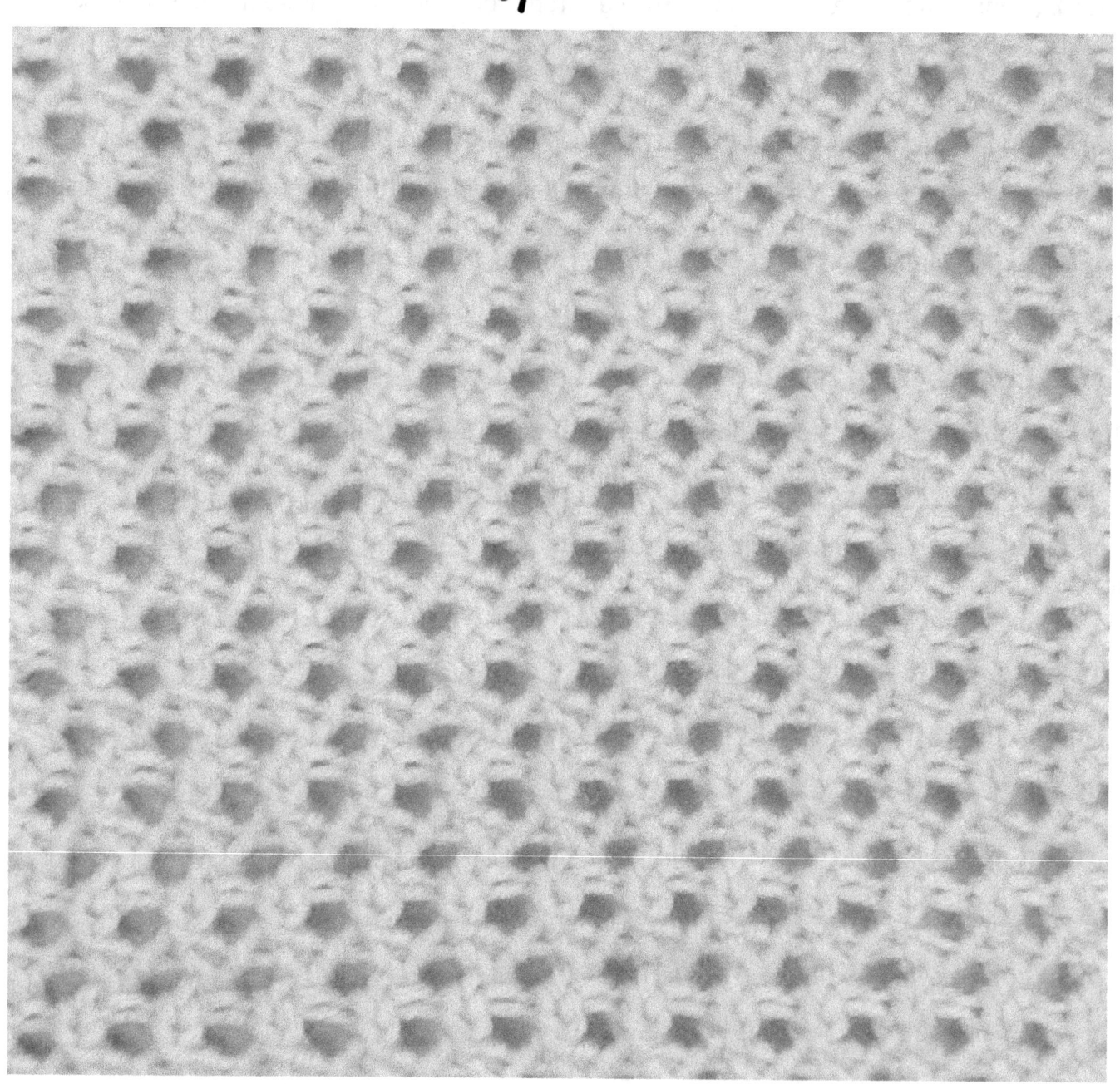

Cast on a multiple of 2, plus 2 edge stitches. Two-stitch repeat. Repeat rows: 1-3. **The edge stitches are not included in the description below and must be added. Slip the first edge stitch, purl the last one.**

**Knit through the back leg, purl as follows:** with the working yarn in front of the stitch, insert the right needle through the stitch from back to front, move the working yarn under the right needle and pull it with the needle through the stitch. The purl stitch that is worked this way sets up the knit stitch to be knitted through the back leg. **Needles: U.S. no. 4 (3.5 mm).**

## Description:

**Row 1:** *Yarn over forward (i.e., from yourself), knit 2 together through the back legs* repeat from * to * until the end of the row.

**Row 2:** *Purl 1, knit 1 through the front leg (yarn over of the previous row)* repeat from * to * until the end of the row.

**Row 3:** *Purl 1, knit 1 through the back leg* repeat from * to * until the end of the row.

**Repeat rows: 1-3.**

**Bind off after the last row 3 as follows:** Slip the edge stitch onto the right needle, knit the next 1 through the front leg, insert the left needle through the slipped edge stitch, from left to right, and pass it over the knitted stitch, *now there is 1 stitch on the right needle, knit the next 1 through the front leg (now there are 2 stitches on the right needle), insert the left needle through the 1st stitch on the right needle, from left to right, and pass it over the 2nd one* repeat from * to * until the end of the row.

# Option 2

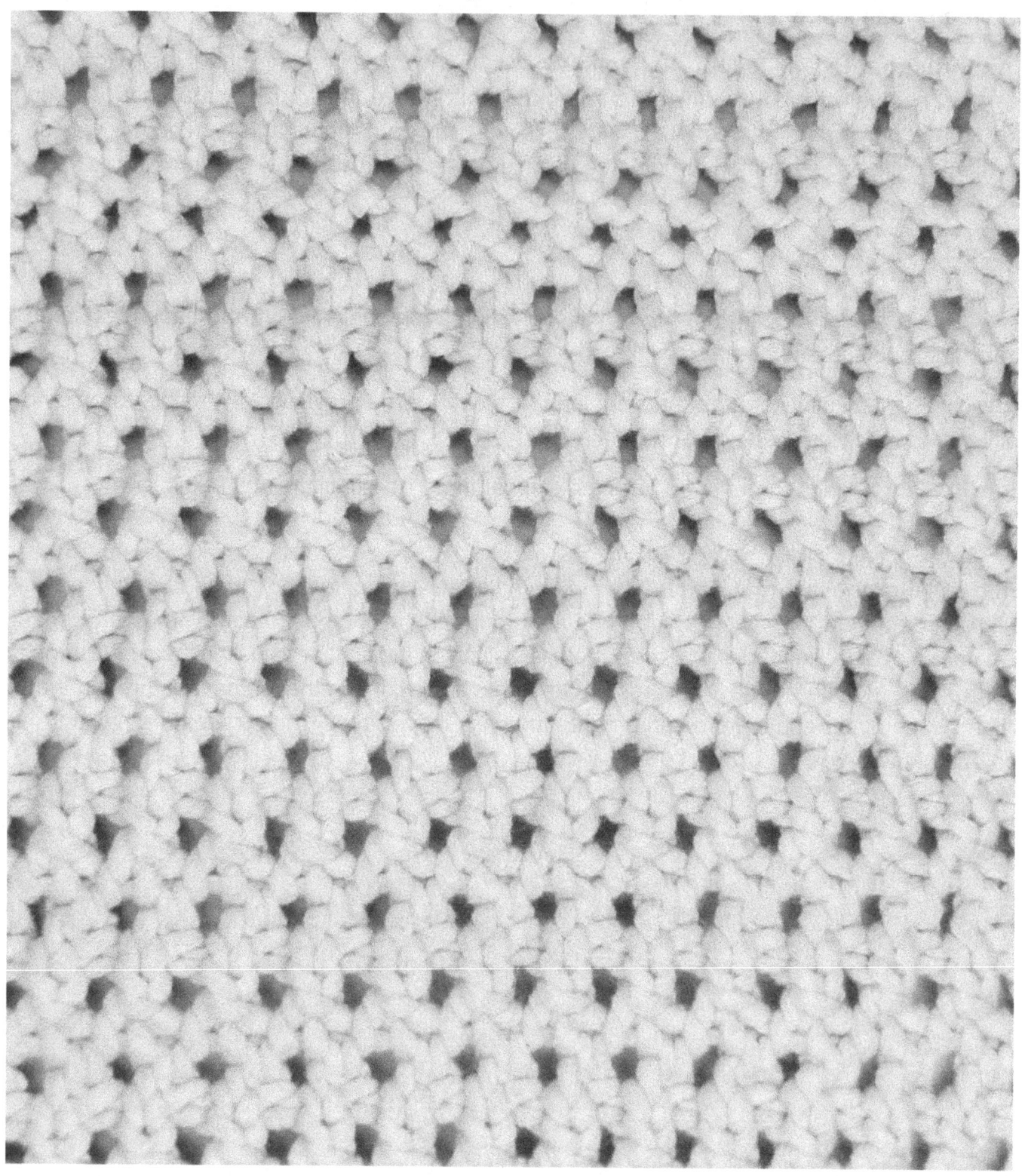

Knit the same as described in option 1 using a bulky yarn. Needles: U.S. no. 7 (4.5 mm).

# Pattern 6

Cast on a multiple of 8, plus 2 edge stitches. Eight-stitch repeat. Repeat rows: 1-4. **The edge stitches are not included in the description below and must be added. Slip the first edge**

stitch; **purl the last one as in knitting through the back leg as follows:** with the working yarn in front of the stitch, insert the right needle through the stitch from back to front, move the working yarn under the right needle and pull it with the needle through the stitch.

**Knit through the front leg, purl as follows:** with the working yarn in front of the stitch, insert the right needle through the stitch from back to front, wrap the working yarn forward (i.e., from yourself) around the tip of the right needle, then pull the working yarn with the right needle through the stitch. The purl stitch that is worked this way sets up the knit stitch to be knitted through the front leg. **Needles: U.S. no. 4 (3.5 mm).**

# Description:

**Row 1 (Back Side):** *Knit 7 out of 1 stitch as follows: knit 1—do not release the left needle yet—yarn over forward (i.e., from yourself), knit 1, yarn over forward, knit 1, yarn over forward, knit 1, then release the left needle, purl the next 7 together* repeat from * to * until the end of the row.

**Row 2 (Front Side):** Purl all the stitches.

**Row 3 (Back Side):** *Purl 7 together, knit 7 out of 1 stitch as described in row 1* repeat from * to * until the end of the row.

**Row 4 (Front Side):** Purl all the stitches.

**Repeat rows:** 1-4.

**Bind off as follows:** After the last row 3, turn your work over; the Front Side: slip all the stitches from the left needle to the right one (as a result, the working yarn is at the end of the row), then turn your work over; the Back Side: slip 2 stitches from the left needle to the right one, insert the left needle through the 1st slipped stitch from left to right and pass it over the 2nd stitch (now, there is 1 stitch on the right needle), *slip 1 from the left needle to the right one, insert the left needle through the 1st stitch on the right needle from left to right and pass it over the 2nd stitch (now, there is 1 stitch on the right needle)* repeat from * to * until the end of the row.

**Note:** For trimming, bind off loosely, using larger needles than the working onesy, as this type of binding off creates a tight chain of small edge stitches that look already finished.

# Pattern 7

Cast on a multiple of 2, plus 2 edge stitches. Two-stitch repeat. Repeat rows: 2-5.

**The edge stitches are not included in the description below and must be added. Slip the first edge stitch; purl the last edge stitch as in knitting through the back leg as follows:** with the working yarn in front of the stitch, insert the right needle through the stitch from back to front, then move the working yarn under the right needle and pull it with the needle through the stitch.

**Knit through the front leg, purl as follows:** with the working yarn in front of the stitch, insert the right needle through the stitch from back to front, wrap the working yarn forward (i.e., from yourself) around the tip of the right needle, then pull the working yarn with the right needle through the stitch. The purl stitch that is worked this way sets up the knit stitch to be knitted through the front leg. **Needles: U.S. no. 7 (4.5 mm) or no. 8 (5 mm). Use a bulky yarn.**

## Description:

**Row 1 (Front Side, set up row):** *Knit 2, yarn over forward (i.e., from yourself)* repeat from * to * until the end of the row.

**Row 2 (Back Side):** *Knit 2 together (1 stitch and yarn over of the previous row), yarn over forward, with the working yarn in front of your work slip the next 1 purlwise* repeat from * to * until the end of the row.

**Row 3 (Front Side):** Knit 1, with the working yarn behind your work, slip 1 purlwise (yarn over of the previous row), *knit 2, with the working yarn behind your work slip 1 purlwise (yarn over of the previous row)* repeat from * to * until the end of the row before the edge stitch, knit 1.

**Row 4 (Back Side):** *Yarn over forward, with the working yarn in front of your work, slip 1 purlwise, knit the next 2 together (1 stitch and yarn over of the previous row)* repeat from * to * until the end of the row.

**Row 5 (Front Side):** *knit 2, with the working yarn behind your work slip 1 purlwise (yarn over of the previous row)* repeat from * to * until the end of the row.

**Repeat rows:** 2-5.

**Bind off as follows:** After the last row 5, turn your work over. The Back Side: slip all the stitches from the left needle to the right one (as a result, the working yarn is at the end of the right needle), then turn your work over. The Front Side: slip 2 purlwise from the left needle to the right one, insert the left needle through the front leg of the 1st slipped stitch, from left to right, and pass it over the 2nd one (now there is 1 stitch on the right needle), *slip 1 purlwise from the left needle to the right one, insert the left needle through the front leg of the 1st stitch on the right needle, from left to right, and pass it over the 2nd one (now there is 1 stitch on the right needle)* repeat from * to * until the end of the row.

# Pattern 8

Cast on a multiple of 2, plus 2 edge stitches. Two-stitch repeat. Repeat rows: 2-5. **The edge stitches are not included in the description below and must be added. Slip the first edge stitch, purl the last one as in knitting through the back leg as follows:** with the working yarn in front of the stitch, insert the right needle through the stitch from back to front, move the working yarn under the right needle and pull it with the needle through the stitch. **Needles: U.S. no. 4 (3.5 mm).**

**Knit through the front leg, purl as follows:** with the working yarn in front of the stitch, insert the right needle through the stitch from back to front, wrap the working yarn forward (i.e., from yourself) around the tip of the right needle, then pull the working yarn with the right needle through the stitch. The purl stitch that is worked this way sets up the knit stitch to be knitted through the front leg.

## Description:

**Row 1 (Back Side, set up row):** *Knit 1 through the front leg, yarn over forward (i.e., from yourself), with the working yarn behind your work slip 1 purlwise* repeat from * to * until the end of the row.

**Row 2 (Front Side):** Knit 1 through the front leg, with the working yarn behind your work, slip 1 purlwise (yarn over of the previous row), *knit 2 through the front legs, with the working yarn behind your work slip 1 purlwise (yarn over of the previous row)* repeat from * to * until the end of the row before the edge stitch, knit 1.

**Row 3 (Back Side):** *Yarn over forward, with the working yarn behind your work, slip 1 purlwise, knit 2 together through the front legs (1 stitch and yarn over of the previous row)* repeat from * to * until the end of the row.

**Row 4 (Front Side):** *Knit 2 through the front legs, with the working yarn behind your work slip 1 purlwise (yarn over of the previous row)* repeat from * to * until the end of the row.

**Row 5 (Back Side):** *Knit 2 together through the front legs (1 stitch and yarn over of the previous row), yarn over forward, with the working yarn behind your work slip 1 purlwise* repeat from * to * until the end of the row.

**Repeat rows:** 2-5.

**Bind off as follows:** After the last row 5, turn your work over. The Front Side: slip all the stitches from the left needle to the right one (as a result, the working yarn is at the end of the right needle);

turn your work over. The Back Side: slip 2 purlwise from the left needle to the right one, insert the left needle through the 1st slipped stitch, from left to right, and pass it over the 2nd one (now there is 1 stitch on the right needle), *slip 1 purlwise from the left needle to the right one, insert the left needle through the 1st stitch on the right needle, from left to right, and pass it over the 2nd one (now there is 1 stitch on the right needle)* repeat from * to * until the end of the row.

**Note:** For trimming, bind off loosely, using larger needles than the working ones, as this type of binding off creates a tight chain of small edge stitches that look already finished.

# Pattern 9
## Reversible

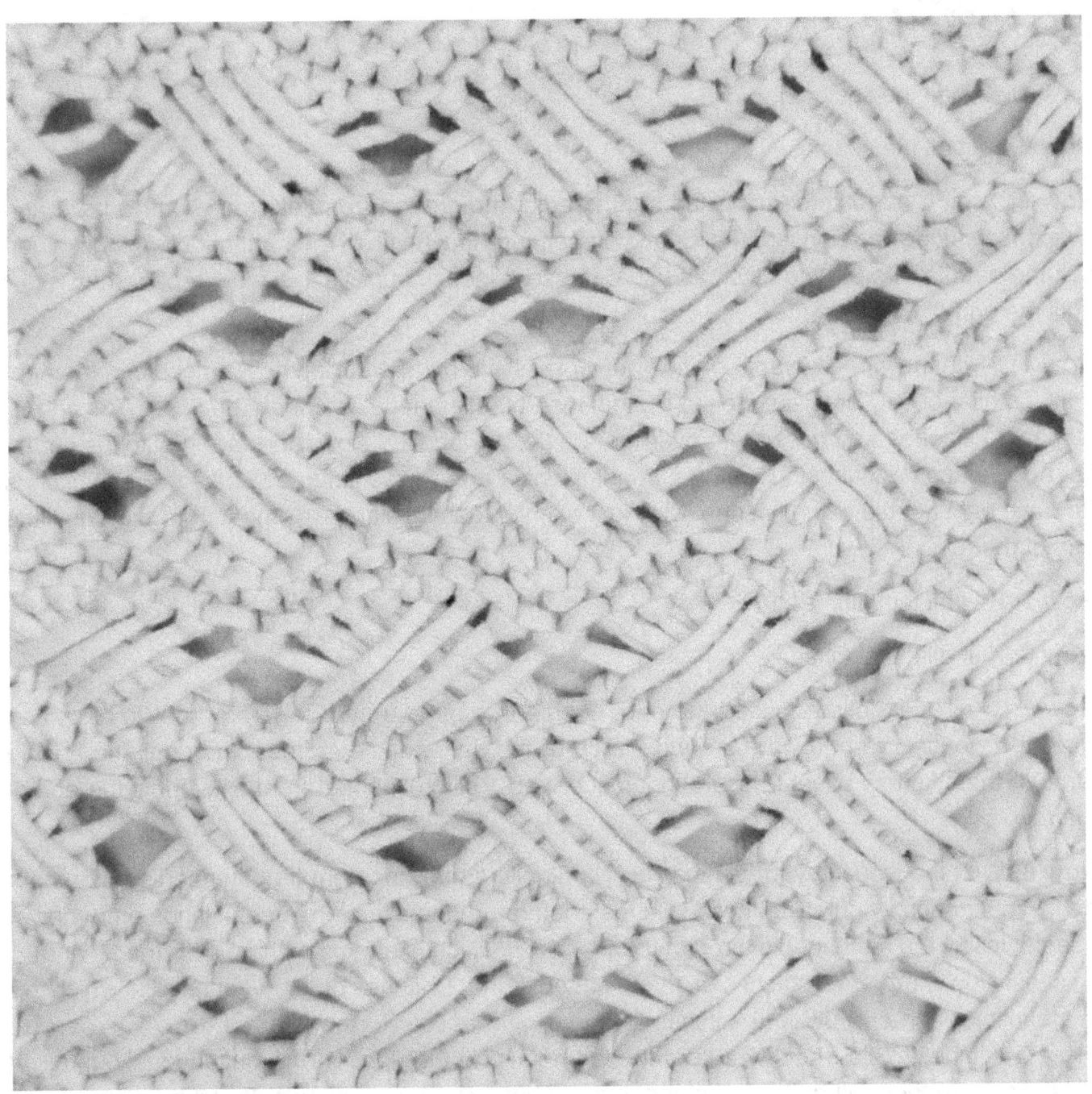

Cast on a multiple of 8, plus 2 edge stitches. Eight-stitch repeat. Repeat rows: 1-8. **The edge stitches are not included in the description below and must be added. Slip the first edge**

**stitch, purl the last one as in knitting through the back leg as follows:** with the working yarn in front of the stitch, insert the right needle through the stitch from back to front, move the working yarn under the right needle and pull it with the needle through the stitch.

**Knit through the front legs. Needles: U.S. no 6 (4 mm). Use a tape yarn or a bulky yarn.**

# Description:

**Row 1:** Knit all the stitches.

**Row 2:** Knit all the stitches.

**Row 3:** *Knit 1 as follows: insert the right needle through the front leg from front to back and wrap the working yarn forward (i.e., from yourself) around the tip of the right needle 4 times, then pull the needle through the stitch as usual (these 4 loops count as 1 stitch)* repeat from * to * until the end of the row.

**Row 4:** *With the working yarn behind your work, slip 8 purlwise from the left needle to the right one, simultaneously unrolling these stitches. Insert the left needle through the 5$^{th}$, 6$^{th}$, 7$^{th}$, and 8$^{th}$ elongated stitches and pass them over the 4$^{th}$, 3$^{rd}$, 2$^{nd}$, and 1$^{st}$. Now there are 4 stitches on the left needle and 4 stitches on the right needle, which are intersecting each other. Slip 4 stitches from the right needle to the left one. Now knit each of these 8 stitches* repeat from * to * until the end of the row.

**Row 5:** Knit all the stitches.

**Row 6:** Knit all the stitches.

**Row 7:** *Knit 1 as follows: insert the right needle through the front leg from front to back and wrap the working yarn forward around the tip of the right needle 4 times, then pull the needle through the stitch as usual (these 4 loops count as 1 stitch)* repeat from * to * until the end of the row.

**Row 8:** With the working yarn behind your work, slip 4 purlwise from the left needle to the right one, simultaneously unrolling these stitches, then return these 4 elongated stitches onto the left needle. Insert the right needle through the 2$^{nd}$ and 1$^{st}$ stitches and pass them over the 3$^{rd}$ and 4$^{th}$ stitches. Now there are 2 stitches on the left needle and 2 stitches on the right needle, which are intersecting each other. Slip 2 stitches from the right needle to the left one. Now knit each of these 4 stitches. *Slip 8 purlwise from the left needle to the right one, simultaneously unrolling these stitches, then return these 8 elongated stitches onto the left needle. Insert the right needle through the 4$^{th}$, 3$^{rd}$, 2$^{nd}$, and 1$^{st}$ elongated stitches and pass them over the 5$^{th}$, 6$^{th}$, 7$^{th}$, and 8$^{th}$ stitches. Now there are 4 stitches on the left needle and 4 stitches on the right needle, which are intersecting each other. Slip 4 stitches from the right needle to the left one. Now knit each of these 8 stitches* repeat from * to * until the end of the row before the edge stitch, work the last 4 stitches the same as the first 4 as follows: Slip 4 purlwise from the left needle to the right one, simultaneously unrolling these stitches, then return these 4 elongated stitches onto the left needle. Insert the right needle through the 2$^{nd}$ and 1$^{st}$ stitches and pass them over the 3$^{rd}$ and 4$^{th}$ stitches. Now there are 2 stitches on the left needle and 2 stitches on the right needle, which are intersecting each other. Slip 2 stitches from the right needle to the left one. Now knit each of these 4 stitches.

**Repeat rows:** 1-8.

**Bind off after the last row 2 as follows:** Slip the edge stitch onto the right needle, knit the next 1 through the front leg, insert the left needle through the slipped edge stitch, from left to right, and pass it over the knitted stitch, *now there is 1 stitch on the right needle, knit the next 1 through the front leg (now there are 2 stitches on the right needle), insert the left needle through the 1$^{st}$ stitch on the right needle, from left to right, and pass it over the 2$^{nd}$ one* repeat from * to * until the end of the row.

# Pattern 10

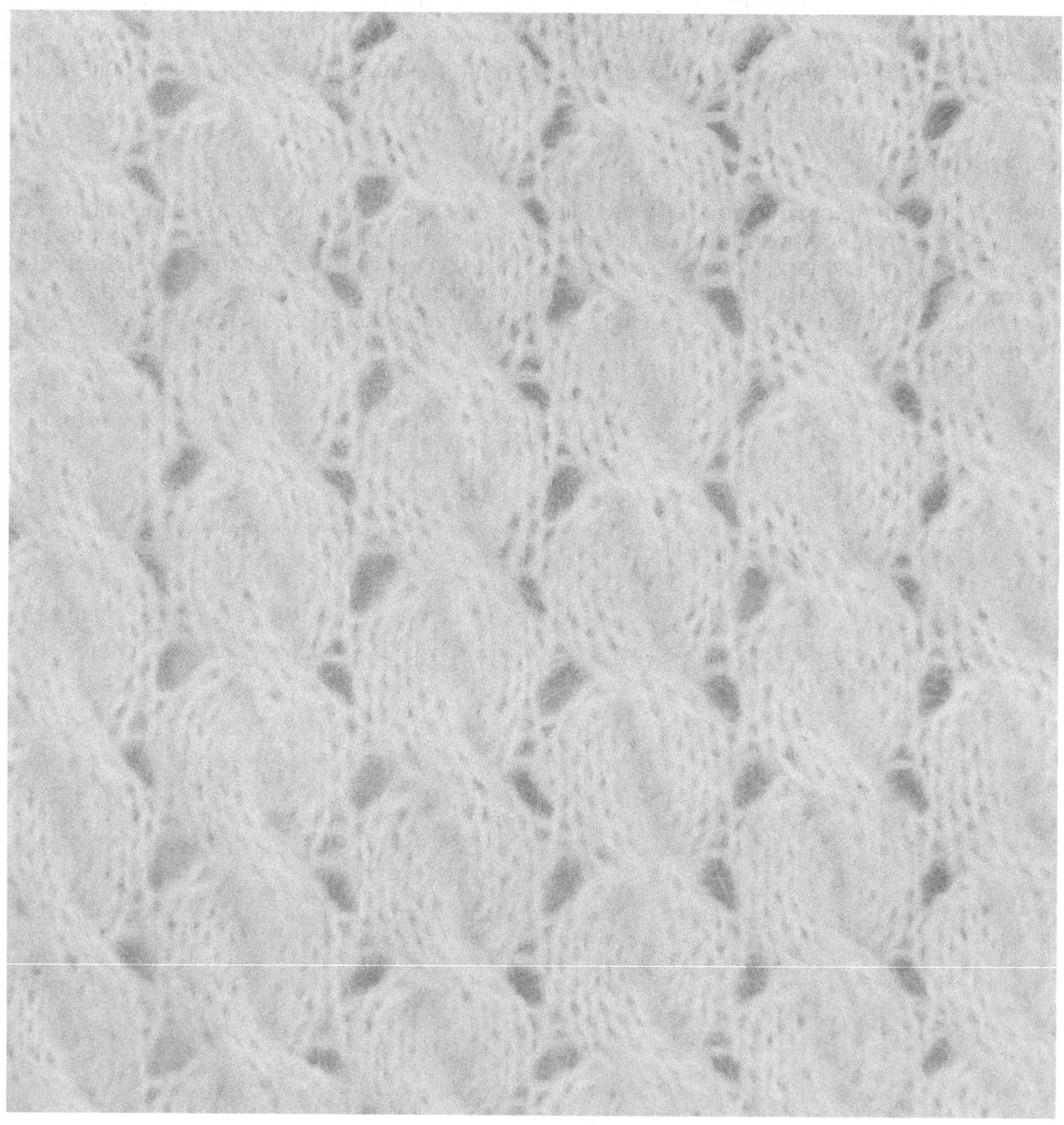

Cast on a multiple of 16, plus 2 edge stitches. Sixteen-stitch repeat. Repeat rows: 1-8.

**The edge stitches are not included in the description below and must be added. Slip the first edge stitch; purl the last edge stitch.**

**Knit through the back leg, purl as follows:** with the working yarn in front of the stitch, insert the right needle through the stitch from back to front, move the working yarn under the right needle and pull it with the needle through the stitch. The purl stitch that is worked this way sets up the knit stitch to be knitted through the back leg.

# Description:

**Row 1:** *Knit 8, yarn over forward (i.e., from yourself), knit 2 together, knit 4, knit 2 together through the front legs as follows: insert the right needle through the 1st stitch from back to front and slip it onto the right needle, insert the right needle through the 2nd stitch from back to front and slip it onto the right needle, then return both stitches onto the left needle, now knit 2 together through front legs, yarn over forward* repeat from * to * until the end of the row.

**Row 2:** Purl all the stitches.

**Row 3:** *Knit 9, slip 3 onto a cable needle in front of your work, knit the next 3, then knit the slipped 3, then knit the next 1* repeat from * to * until the end of the row.

**Row 4:** Purl all the stitches.

**Row 5:** *Yarn over forward, knit 2 together, knit 4, knit 2 together through the front legs as follows: insert the right needle through the 1st stitch from back to front and slip it onto the right needle, insert the right needle through the 2nd stitch from back to front and slip it onto the right needle, then return both stitches onto the left needle, now knit 2 together through the front legs, then yarn over forward, knit 8* repeat from * to * until the end of the row.

**Row 6:** Purl all the stitches.

**Row 7:** *Knit 1, slip 3 onto a cable needle in front of your work, knit the next 3, then knit the slipped 3, knit 9* repeat from * to * until the end of the row.

**Row 8:** Purl all the stitches.

**Repeat rows:** 1-8.

**Bind off after the last row 8 as follows:** Slip the edge stitch onto the right needle, knit the next 1 through the back leg, insert the left needle through the slipped edge stitch, from left to right, and pass it over the knitted stitch, *now there is 1 stitch on the right needle, knit the next 1 through the back leg (now there are 2 stitches on the right needle), insert the left needle through the 1st stitch on the right needle, from left to right, and pass it over the 2nd one* repeat from * to * until the end of the row.

# Pattern 11

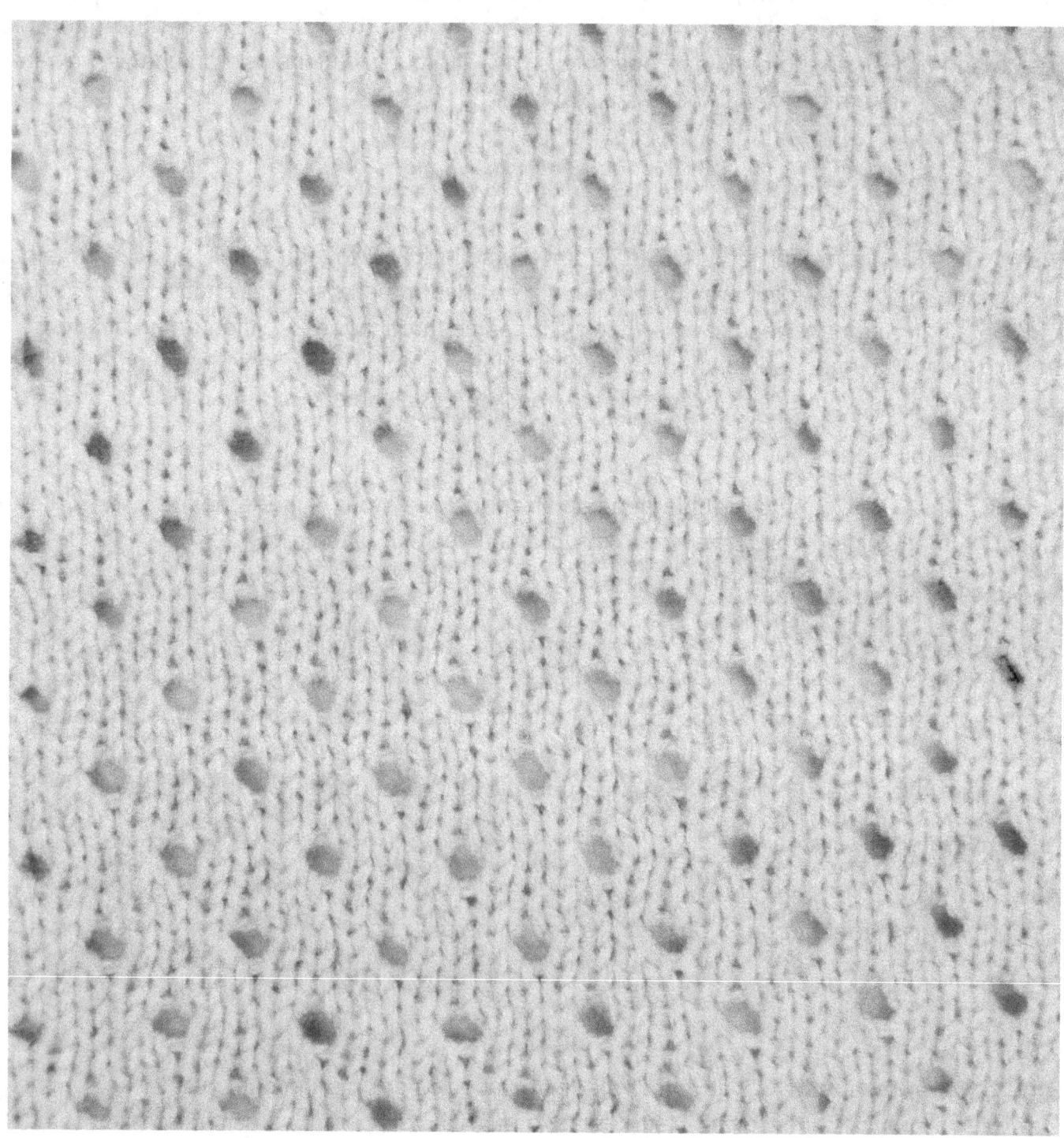

Cast on a multiple of 4, plus 1 for symmetry, and 2 edge stitches. Four-stitch repeat. Repeat rows: 1-8. **The edge stitches are not included in the description below and must be added. Slip the first edge stitch; purl the last edge stitch.**

**Knit through the back leg, purl as follows:** with the working yarn in front of the stitch, insert the right needle through the stitch from back to front, move the working yarn under the right needle and pull it with the needle through the stitch. The purl stitch that is worked this way sets up the knit stitch to be knitted through the back leg. **Needles: U.S. no. 4 (3.5 mm).**

# Description:

**Row 1:** Knit 1, *knit 2, yarn over forward (i.e., from yourself), knit 2 together through the front legs as follows: slip 1 onto the right needle purlwise, slip the next 1 onto the right needle, inserting the right needle through the back leg from back to front, thus moving the back leg to the front, then return both stitches onto the left needle, now knit 2 together through the front legs* repeat from * to * until the end of the row.

**Row 2:** Purl all the stitches.

**Row 3:** Knit all the stitches.

**Row 4:** Purl all the stitches.

**Row 5:** Knit 1, *yarn over forward, knit 2 together through the front legs as follows: slip 1 onto the right needle purlwise, slip the next 1 onto the right needle, inserting the right needle through the back leg from back to front, thus moving the back leg to the front, then return both stitches onto the left needle, now knit 2 together through the front legs, knit 2* repeat from * to * until the end of the row.

**Row 6:** Purl all the stitches.

**Row 7:** Knit all the stitches.

**Row 8:** Purl all the stitches.

**Repeat rows: 1-8.**

**Bind off after the last row 6 as follows:** Slip the edge stitch onto the right needle, knit the next 1, insert the left needle through the slipped edge stitch, from left to right, and pass it over the knitted stitch, *now there is 1 stitch on the right needle, knit the next 1 (now there are 2 stitches on the right needle), insert the left needle through the 1st stitch on the right needle, from left to right, and pass it over the 2nd one* repeat from * to * until the end of the row.

# Pattern 12

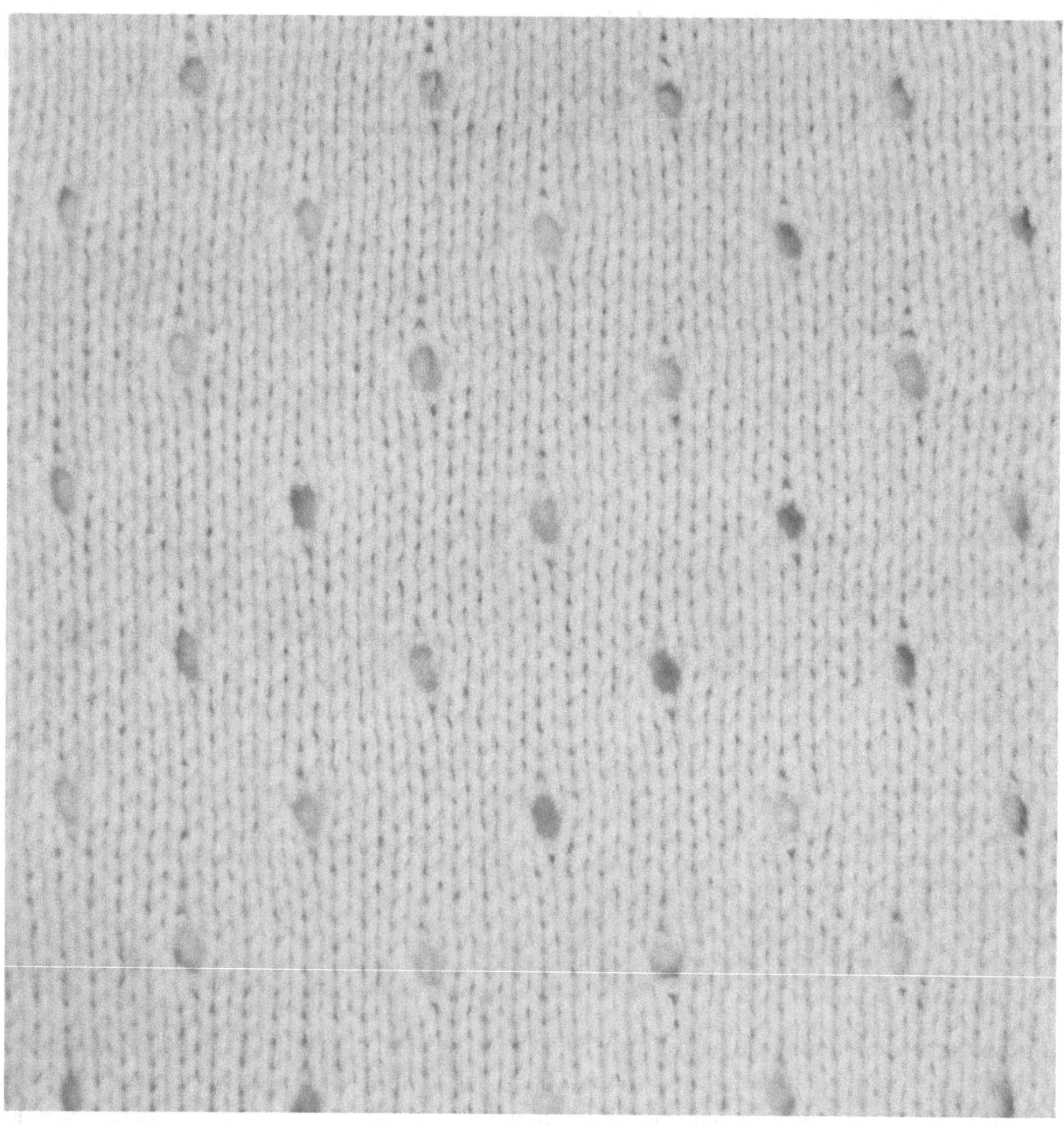

Cast on a multiple of 8, plus 2 edge stitches. Eight-stitch repeat. Repeat rows: 1-12.

**The edge stitches are not included in the description below and must be added. Slip the first edge stitch; purl the last edge stitch.**

**Knit through the back leg, purl as follows:** with the working yarn in front of the stitch, insert the right needle through the stitch from back to front, move the working yarn under the right needle and pull it with the needle through the stitch. The purl stitch that is worked this way sets up the knit stitch to be knitted through the back leg. **Needles: U.S. no. 4 (3.5 mm).**

# Description:

**Row 1:** *Knit 3, yarn over forward (i.e., from yourself), knit 2 together through the front legs as follows: slip 1 onto the right needle purlwise, slip the next 1 onto the right needle, inserting the right needle through the back leg from back to front, thus turning the back leg to the front, then return both stitches onto the left needle, now knit 2 together through the front legs, knit 3* repeat from * to * until the end of the row.

**Row 2:** Purl all the stitches.

**Row 3:** Knit all the stitches.

**Row 4:** Purl all the stitches.

**Row 5:** Knit all the stitches.

**Row 6:** Purl all the stitches.

**Row 7:** Knit 4, *knit 3, yarn over forward, knit 2 together through the front legs as follows: slip 1 onto the right needle purlwise, slip the next 1 onto the right needle, inserting the right needle through the back leg from back to front, thus turning the back leg to the front, then return both stitches onto the left needle, now knit 2 together through the front legs, knit 3* repeat from * to * until the end of the row before the edge stitch, knit 4.

**Row 8:** Purl all the stitches.

**Row 9:** Knit all the stitches.

**Row 10:** Purl all the stitches.

**Row 11:** Knit all the stitches.

**Row 12:** Purl all the stitches.

**Repeat rows:** 1-12.

**Bind off after the last row 8 as follows:** Slip the edge stitch onto the right needle, knit the next 1 through the back leg, insert the left needle through the slipped edge stitch, from left to right, and pass it over the knitted stitch, *now there is 1 stitch on the right needle, knit the next 1 through the back leg (now there are 2 stitches on the right needle), insert the left needle through the 1st stitch on the right needle, from left to right, and pass it over the 2nd one* repeat from * to * until the end of the row.

# Pattern 13

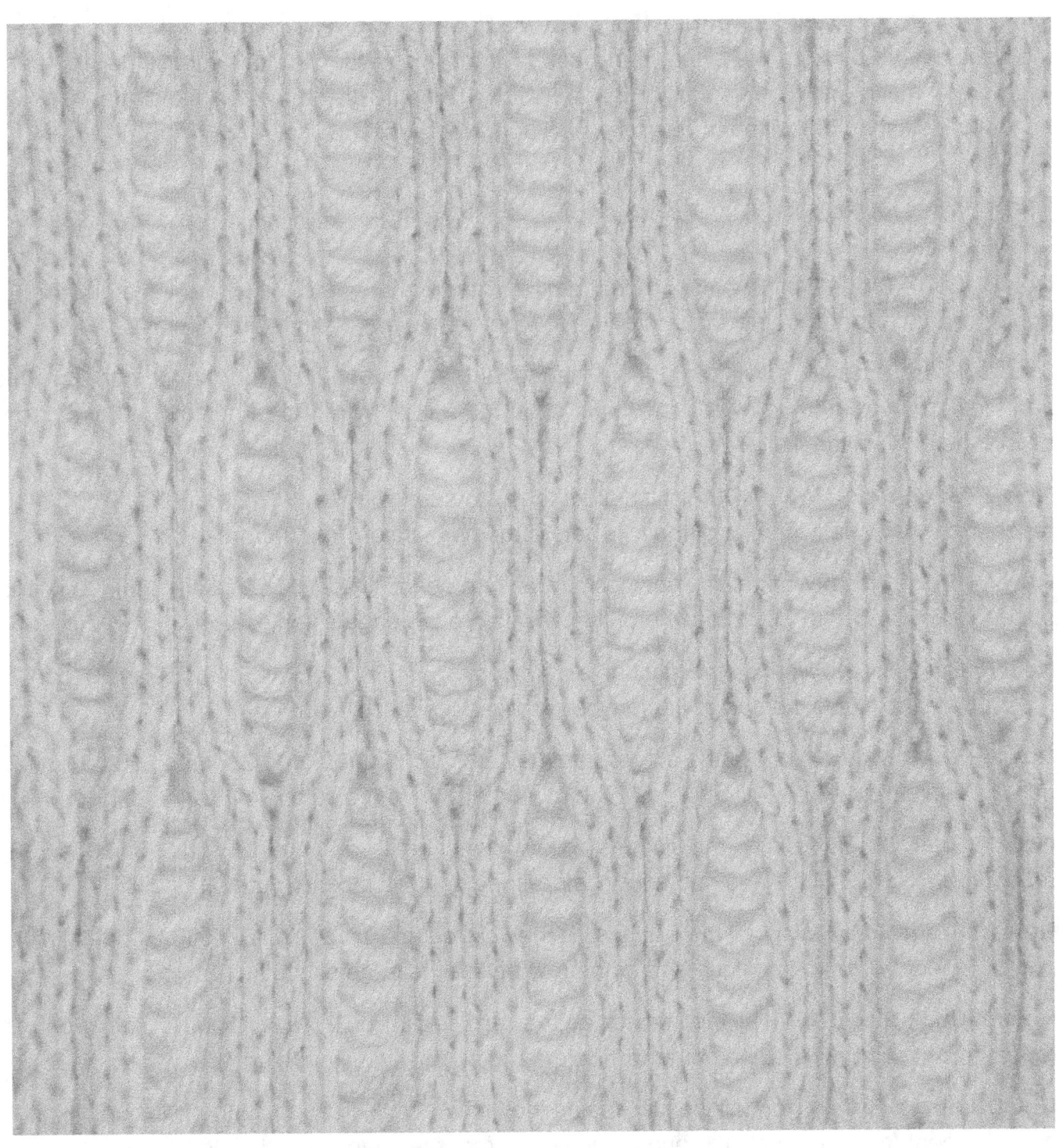

Cast on a multiple of 8, plus 6 for symmetry, and 2 edge stitches. Eight-stitch repeat. Repeat rows: 13-36. **The edge stitches are not included in the description below and must be added. Slip the first edge stitch; purl the last edge stitch.**

**Knit through the back leg, purl as follows:** with the working yarn in front of the stitch, insert the right needle through the stitch from back to front, move the working yarn under the right needle and pull it with the needle through the stitch. The purl stitch that is worked this way sets up the knit stitch to be knitted through the back leg. **Needles: U.S. no. 4 (3.5 mm).**

## Description:

**Row 1 (Back Side):** Purl 2, *knit 2, purl 2, knit 1, yarn over forward (i.e., from yourself), knit 1, purl 2* repeat from * to * until the end of the row before the edge stitch, knit 2, purl 2.

**Row 2 (Front Side):** Work all the stitches as they are seen: Knit 2, purl 2, *knit 2, purl 3 (**note:** purl the yarn over of the previous row), knit 2, purl 2* repeat from * to * until the end of the row before the edge stitch, knit 2.

**Row 3 (Back Side):** Work all the stitches as they are seen: Purl 2, *knit 2, purl 2, knit 3, purl 2* repeat from * to * until the end of the row before the edge stitch, knit 2, purl 2.

**Row 4 (Front Side):** Work all the stitches as they are seen: Knit 2, purl 2, *knit 2, purl 3, knit 2, purl 2* repeat from * to * until the end of the row before the edge stitch, knit 2.

**Row 5 (Back Side):** Work all the stitches as they are seen: Purl 2, *knit 2, purl 2, knit 3, purl 2* repeat from * to * until the end of the row before the edge stitch, knit 2, purl 2.

**Row 6 (Front Side):** Work all the stitches as they are seen: Knit 2, purl 2, *knit 2, purl 3, knit 2, purl 2* repeat from * to * until the end of the row before the edge stitch, knit 2.

**Row 7 (Back Side):** Work all the stitches as they are seen: Purl 2, *knit 2, purl 2, knit 3, purl 2* repeat from * to * until the end of the row before the edge stitch, knit 2, purl 2.

**Row 8 (Front Side):** Work all the stitches as they are seen: Knit 2, purl 2, *knit 2, purl 3, knit 2, purl 2* repeat from * to * until the end of the row before the edge stitch, knit 2.

**Row 9 (Back Side):** Work all the stitches as they are seen: Purl 2, *knit 2, purl 2, knit 3, purl 2* repeat from * to * until the end of the row before the edge stitch, knit 2, purl 2.

**Row 10 (Front Side):** Work all the stitches as they are seen: Knit 2, purl 2, *knit 2, purl 3, knit 2, purl 2* repeat from * to * until the end of the row before the edge stitch, knit 2.

**Row 11 (Back Side):** Work all the stitches as they are seen: Purl 2, *knit 2, purl 2, knit 3, purl 2* repeat from * to * until the end of the row before the edge stitch, knit 2, purl 2.

**Row 12 (Front Side):** Work all the stitches as they are seen: Knit 2, purl 2, *knit 2, purl 3, knit 2, purl 2* repeat from * to * until the end of the row before the edge stitch, knit 2.

**Row 13 (Back Side):** Purl 2, *knit 1, yarn over forward, knit 1, purl 2, knit 1, slip the next 1 off the left needle and leave it as is, knit the next 1, purl 2* repeat from * to * until the end of the row before the edge stitch, knit 1, yarn over forward, knit 1, purl 2. **Slide down the slipped stitches until the row in which these yarn overs were made.**

**Row 14 (Front Side):** Work all the stitches as they are seen: Knit 2, purl 3 (purl the yarn over of the previous row), *knit 2, purl 2, knit 2, purl 3* repeat from * to * until the end of the row before the edge stitch, knit 2.

**Row 15 (Back Side):** Work all the stitches as they are seen: Purl 2, *knit 3, purl 2, knit 2, purl 2* repeat from * to * until the end of the row before the edge stitch, knit 3, purl 2.

**Row 16 (Front Side):** Work all the stitches as they are seen: Knit 2, purl 3, *knit 2, purl 2, knit 2, purl 3* repeat from * to * until the end of the row before the edge stitch, knit 2.

**Row 17 (Back Side):** Work all the stitches as they are seen: Purl 2, *knit 3, purl 2, knit 2, purl 2* repeat from * to * until the end of the row before the edge stitch, knit 3, purl 2.

**Row 18 (Front Side):** Work all the stitches as they are seen: Knit 2, purl 3, *knit 2, purl 2, knit 2, purl 3* repeat from * to * until the end of the row, before the edge stitch, knit 2.

**Row 19 (Back Side):** Work all the stitches as they are seen: Purl 2, *knit 3, purl 2, knit 2, purl 2* repeat from * to * until the end of the row before the edge stitch, knit 3, purl 2.

**Row 20 (Front Side):** Work all the stitches as they are seen: Knit 2, purl 3, *knit 2, purl 2, knit 2, purl 3* repeat from * to * until the end of the row before the edge stitch, knit 2.

**Row 21 (Back Side):** Work all the stitches as they are seen: Purl 2, *knit 3, purl 2, knit 2, purl 2* repeat from * to * until the end of the row before the edge stitch, knit 3, purl 2.

**Row 22 (Front Side):** Work all the stitches as they are seen: Knit 2, purl 3, *knit 2, purl 2, knit 2, purl 3* repeat from * to * until the end of the row before the edge stitch, knit 2.

**Row 23 (Back Side):** Work all the stitches as they are seen: Purl 2, *knit 3, purl 2, knit 2, purl 2* repeat from * to * until the end of the row before the edge stitch, knit 3, purl 2.

**Row 24 (Front Side):** Work all the stitches as they are seen: Knit 2, purl 3, *knit 2, purl 2, knit 2, purl 3* repeat from * to * until the end of the row before the edge stitch, knit 2.

**Row 25 (Back Side):** Purl 2, *knit 1, slip one off the left needle and leave it as is, knit the next 1, purl 2, knit 1, yarn over forward, knit 1, purl 2 * repeat from * to * until the end of the row before the edge stitch, the last 5 stitches, knit 1, slip one off the left needle and leave it as is, knit the next 1, purl 2. **Slide down the slipped stitches until the row in which these yarn overs were made.**

**Row 26 (Front Side):** Work all the stitches as they are seen: Knit 2, purl 2, *knit 2, purl 3 (purl yarn over of the previous row), knit 2, purl 2* repeat from * to * until the end of the row before the edge stitch, knit 2.

**Row 27 (Back Side):** Work all the stitches as they are seen: Purl 2, *knit 2, purl 2, knit 3, purl 2* repeat from * to * until the end of the row before the edge stitch, knit 2, purl 2.

**Row 28 (Front Side):** Work all the stitches as they are seen: Knit 2, purl 2, *knit 2, purl 3, knit 2, purl 2* repeat from * to * until the end of the row before the edge stitch, knit 2.

**Row 29 (Back Side):** Work all the stitches as they are seen: Purl 2, *knit 2, purl 2, knit 3, purl 2* repeat from * to * until the end of the row before the edge stitch, knit 2, purl 2.

**Row 30 (Front Side):** Work all the stitches as they are seen: Knit 2, purl 2, *knit 2, purl 3, knit 2, purl 2* repeat from * to * until the end of the row before the edge stitch, knit 2.

**Row 31 (Back Side):** Work all the stitches as they are seen: Purl 2, *knit 2, purl 2, knit 3, purl 2* repeat from * to * until the end of the row before the edge stitch, knit 2, purl 2.

**Row 32 (Front Side):** Work all the stitches as they are seen: Knit 2, purl 2, *knit 2, purl 3, knit 2, purl 2* repeat from * to * until the end of the row before the edge stitch, knit 2.

**Row 33 (Back Side):** Work all the stitches as they are seen: Purl 2, *knit 2, purl 2, knit 3, purl 2* repeat from * to * until the end of the row before the edge stitch, knit 2, purl 2.

**Row 34 (Front Side):** Work all the stitches as they are seen: Knit 2, purl 2, *knit 2, purl 3, knit 2, purl 2* repeat from * to * until the end of the row before the edge stitch, knit 2.

**Row 35 (Back Side):** Work all the stitches as they are seen: Purl 2, *knit 2, purl 2, knit 3, purl 2* repeat from * to * until the end of the row before the edge stitch, knit 2, purl 2.

**Row 36 (Front Side):** Work all the stitches as they are seen: Knit 2, purl 2, *knit 2, purl 3, knit 2, purl 2* repeat from * to * until the end of the row before the edge stitch, knit 2.

**Row 37 (Back Side):** Repeat row 13, etc.

**Repeat rows:** 13-36.

**Note: Bind off after the last row 13 (or the last row 25). In the last row 13 (or 25), slip the knit stitches off the left needle, following instructions as usual, but do not make yarn overs between 2 knit stitches in this row, to avoid holes in the edge row.**

**Bind off as follows:** After the last row 13 (or 25), turn your work over. The Front Side: slip all the stitches from the left needle to the right one (as a result, the working yarn is at the end of the right needle); turn your work over. The Back Side: slip 2 purlwise from the left needle to the right one, insert the left needle through the 1st slipped stitch, from left to right, and pass it over the 2nd one (now there is 1 stitch on the right needle), *slip 1 purlwise from the left needle to the right one, insert the left needle through the 1st stitch on the right needle, from left to right, and pass it over the 2nd one (now there is 1 stitch on the right needle)* repeat from * to * until the end of the row.

**Note:** For trimming, bind off loosely, using larger needles than the working ones, as this type of binding off creates a tight chain of small edge stitches that look already finished.

# Pattern 14

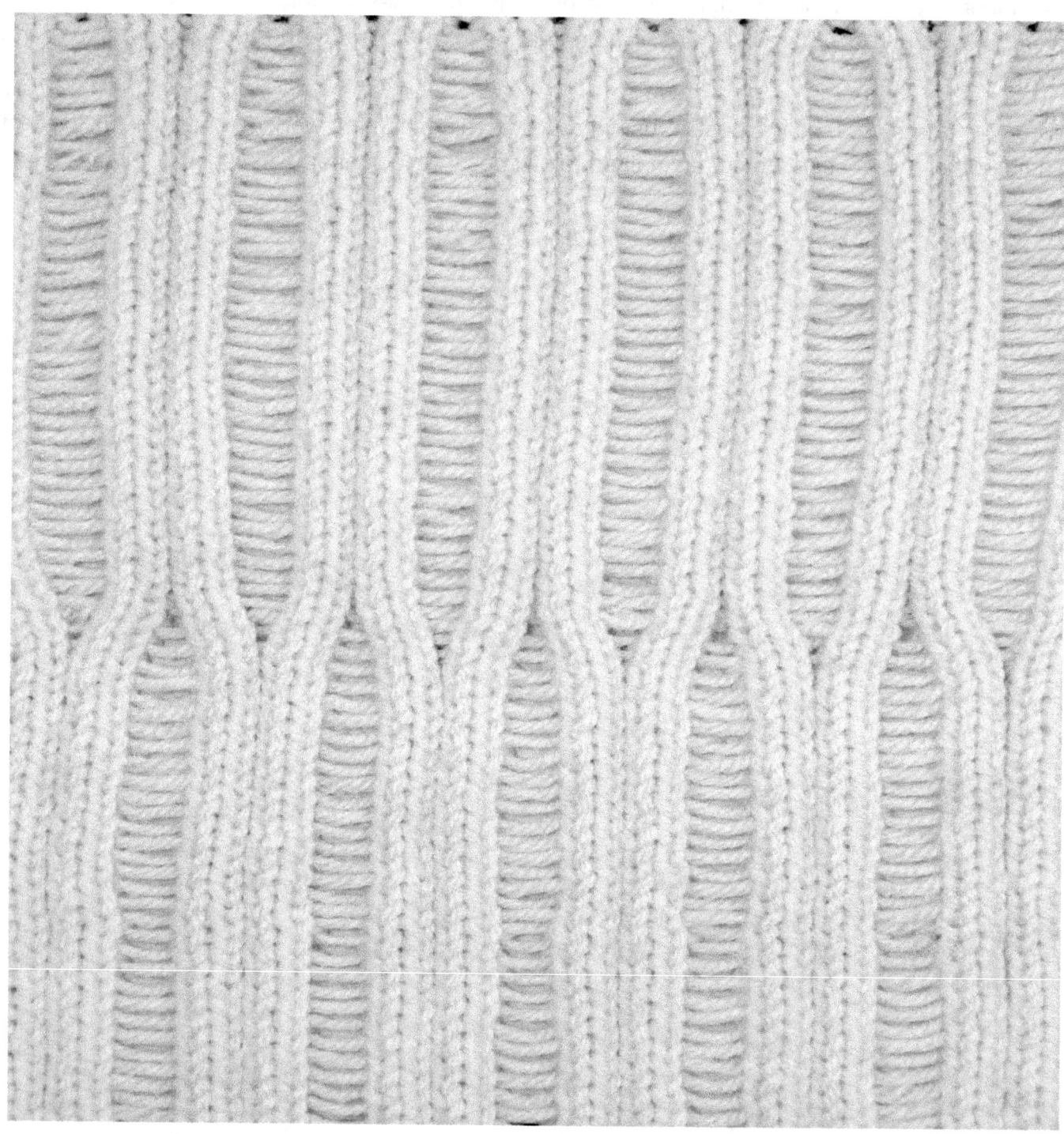

Cast on a multiple of 8, plus 6 for symmetry, and 2 edge stitches. Eight-stitch repeat. Repeat rows: 3-82. **The edge stitches are not included in the description below and must be added. Slip the first edge stitch, purl the last one.**

**Knit through the back leg, purl as follows:** with the working yarn in front of the stitch, insert the right needle through the stitch from back to front, move the working yarn under the right needle and pull it with the needle through the stitch. The purl stitch that is worked this way sets up the knit stitch to be knitted through the back leg. **Needles: U.S. no. 4 (3.5 mm).**

# Description:

**Row 1 (set up row, Back Side):** Purl 2, *knit 2, purl 2, knit 1, yarn over forward (i.e., from yourself), knit 1, purl 2* repeat from * to * before the edge stitch, knit 2, purl 2.

**Row 2 (set up row, Front Side):** Work all the stitches as they are seen: Knit 2, purl 2, *knit 2, purl 3 (purl yarn over of the previous row), knit 2, purl 2* repeat from * to * until the end of the row before the edge stitch, knit 2.

**Row 3 (Back Side):** Work all the stitches as they are seen: Purl 2, *knit 2, purl 2, knit 3, purl 2* repeat from * to * until the end of the row before the edge stitch, knit 2, purl 2.

**Row 4 (Front Side):** Work all the stitches as they are seen: Knit 2, purl 2, *knit 2, purl 3, knit 2, purl 2* repeat from * to * until the end of the row before the edge stitch, knit 2.

**Row 5 (Back Side):** Work all the stitches as they are seen: Purl 2, *knit 2, purl 2, knit 3, purl 2* repeat from * to * until the end of the row before the edge stitch, knit 2, purl 2.

**Row 6 (Front Side):** Work all the stitches as they are seen: Knit 2, purl 2, *knit 2, purl 3, knit 2, purl 2* repeat from * to * until the end of the row before the edge stitch, knit 2.

**Row 7 (Back Side):** Work all the stitches as they are seen: Purl 2, *knit 2, purl 2, knit 3, purl 2* repeat from * to * until the end of the row before the edge stitch, knit 2, purl 2.

**Row 8 (Front Side):** Work all the stitches as they are seen: Knit 2, purl 2, *knit 2, purl 3, knit 2, purl 2* repeat from * to * until the end of the row before the edge stitch, knit 2.

**Row 9 (Back Side):** Work all the stitches as they are seen: Purl 2, *knit 2, purl 2, knit 3, purl 2* repeat from * to * until the end of the row before the edge stitch, knit 2, purl 2.

**Row 10 (Front Side):** Work all the stitches as they are seen: Knit 2, purl 2, *knit 2, purl 3, knit 2, purl 2* repeat from * to * until the end of the row before the edge stitch, knit 2.

**Row 11 (Back Side):** Work all the stitches as they are seen: Purl 2, *knit 2, purl 2, knit 3, purl 2* repeat from * to * until the end of the row before the edge stitch, knit 2, purl 2.

**Row 12 (Front Side):** Work all the stitches as they are seen: Knit 2, purl 2, *knit 2, purl 3, knit 2, purl 2* repeat from * to * until the end of the row before the edge stitch, knit 2.

**Row 13 (Back Side):** Work all the stitches as they are seen: Purl 2, *knit 2, purl 2, knit 3, purl 2* repeat from * to * until the end of the row before the edge stitch, knit 2, purl 2.

**Row 14 (Front Side):** Work all the stitches as they are seen: Knit 2, purl 2, *knit 2, purl 3, knit 2, purl 2* repeat from * to * until the end of the row before the edge stitch, knit 2.

**Row 15 (Back Side):** Work all the stitches as they are seen: Purl 2, *knit 2, purl 2, knit 3, purl 2* repeat from * to * until the end of the row before the edge stitch, knit 2, purl 2.

**Row 16 (Front Side):** Work all the stitches as they are seen: Knit 2, purl 2, *knit 2, purl 3, knit 2, purl 2* repeat from * to * until the end of the row before the edge stitch, knit 2.

**Row 17 (Back Side):** Work all the stitches as they are seen: Purl 2, *knit 2, purl 2, knit 3, purl 2* repeat from * to * until the end of the row before the edge stitch, knit 2, purl 2.

**Row 18 (Front Side):** Work all the stitches as they are seen: Knit 2, purl 2, *knit 2, purl 3, knit 2, purl 2* repeat from * to * until the end of the row before the edge stitch, knit 2.

**Row 19 (Back Side):** Work all the stitches as they are seen: Purl 2, *knit 2, purl 2, knit 3, purl 2* repeat from * to * until the end of the row before the edge stitch, knit 2, purl 2.

**Row 20 (Front Side):** Work all the stitches as they are seen: Knit 2, purl 2, *knit 2, purl 3, knit 2, purl 2* repeat from * to * until the end of the row before the edge stitch, knit 2.

**Row 21 (Back Side):** Work all the stitches as they are seen: Purl 2, *knit 2, purl 2, knit 3, purl 2* repeat from * to * until the end of the row before the edge stitch, knit 2, purl 2.

**Row 22 (Front Side):** Work all the stitches as they are seen: Knit 2, purl 2, *knit 2, purl 3, knit 2, purl 2* repeat from * to * until the end of the row before the edge stitch, knit 2.

**Row 23 (Back Side):** Work all the stitches as they are seen: Purl 2, *knit 2, purl 2, knit 3, purl 2* repeat from * to * until the end of the row before the edge stitch, knit 2, purl 2.

**Row 24 (Front Side):** Work all the stitches as they are seen: Knit 2, purl 2, *knit 2, purl 3, knit 2, purl 2* repeat from * to * until the end of the row before the edge stitch, knit 2.

**Row 25 (Back Side):** Work all the stitches as they are seen: Purl 2, *knit 2, purl 2, knit 3, purl 2* repeat from * to * until the end of the row before the edge stitch, knit 2, purl 2.

**Row 26 (Front Side):** Work all the stitches as they are seen: Knit 2, purl 2, *knit 2, purl 3, knit 2, purl 2* repeat from * to * until the end of the row before the edge stitch, knit 2.

**Row 27 (Back Side):** Work all the stitches as they are seen: Purl 2, *knit 2, purl 2, knit 3, purl 2* repeat from * to * until the end of the row before the edge stitch, knit 2, purl 2.

**Row 28 (Front Side):** Work all the stitches as they are seen: Knit 2, purl 2, *knit 2, purl 3, knit 2, purl 2* repeat from * to * until the end of the row before the edge stitch, knit 2.

**Row 29 (Back Side):** Work all the stitches as they are seen: Purl 2, *knit 2, purl 2, knit 3, purl 2* repeat from * to * until the end of the row before the edge stitch, knit 2, purl 2.

**Row 30 (Front Side):** Work all the stitches as they are seen: Knit 2, purl 2, *knit 2, purl 3, knit 2, purl 2* repeat from * to * until the end of the row before the edge stitch, knit 2.

**Row 31 (Back Side):** Work all the stitches as they are seen: Purl 2, *knit 2, purl 2, knit 3, purl 2* repeat from * to * until the end of the row before the edge stitch, knit 2, purl 2.

**Row 32 (Front Side):** Work all the stitches as they are seen: Knit 2, purl 2, *knit 2, purl 3, knit 2, purl 2* repeat from * to * until the end of the row before the edge stitch, knit 2.

**Row 33 (Back Side):** Work all the stitches as they are seen: Purl 2, *knit 2, purl 2, knit 3, purl 2* repeat from * to * until the end of the row before the edge stitch, knit 2, purl 2.

**Row 34 (Front Side):** Work all the stitches as they are seen: Knit 2, purl 2, *knit 2, purl 3, knit 2, purl 2* repeat from * to * until the end of the row before the edge stitch, knit 2.

**Row 35 (Back Side):** Work all the stitches as they are seen: Purl 2, *knit 2, purl 2, knit 3, purl 2* repeat from * to * until the end of the row before the edge stitch, knit 2, purl 2.

**Row 36 (Front Side):** Work all the stitches as they are seen: Knit 2, purl 2, *knit 2, purl 3, knit 2, purl 2* repeat from * to * until the end of the row before the edge stitch, knit 2.

**Row 37 (Back Side):** Work all the stitches as they are seen: Purl 2, *knit 2, purl 2, knit 3, purl 2* repeat from * to * until the end of the row before the edge stitch, knit 2, purl 2.

**Row 38 (Front Side):** Work all the stitches as they are seen: Knit 2, purl 2, *knit 2, purl 3, knit 2, purl 2* repeat from * to * until the end of the row before the edge stitch, knit 2.

**Row 39 (Back Side):** Work all the stitches as they are seen: Purl 2, *knit 2, purl 2, knit 3, purl 2* repeat from * to * until the end of the row before the edge stitch, knit 2, purl 2.

**Row 40 (Front Side):** Work all the stitches as they are seen: Knit 2, purl 2, *knit 2, purl 3, knit 2, purl 2* repeat from * to * until the end of the row before the edge stitch, knit 2.

**Row 41 (Back Side):** Purl 2, *knit 1, yarn over forward, knit 1, purl 2, knit 1, slip the next 1 off the left needle and leave it as is, knit the next 1, purl 2* repeat from * to * until the end of the row before the edge stitch, knit 1, yarn over forward, knit 1, purl 2. **Slide down the slipped stitches until the row in which the yarn overs were made.**

**Row 42 (Front Side):** Work all the stitches as they are seen: Knit 2, purl 3 (purl yarn over of the previous row), *knit 2, purl 2, knit 2, purl 3* repeat from * to * until the end of the row before the edge stitch, knit 2.

**Row 43 (Back Side):** Work all the stitches as they are seen: Purl 2, *knit 3, purl 2, knit 2, purl 2* repeat from * to * until the end of the row before the edge stitch, knit 3, purl 2.

**Row 44 (Front Side):** Work all the stitches as they are seen: Knit 2, purl 3, *knit 2, purl 2, knit 2, purl 3* repeat from * to * until the end of the row before the edge stitch, knit 2.

**Row 45 (Back Side):** Work all the stitches as they are seen: Purl 2, *knit 3, purl 2, knit 2, purl 2* repeat from * to * until the end of the row before the edge stitch, knit 3, purl 2.

**Row 46 (Front Side):** Work all the stitches as they are seen: Knit 2, purl 3, *knit 2, purl 2, knit 2, purl 3* repeat from * to * until the end of the row, before the edge stitch, knit 2.

**Row 47 (Back Side):** Work all the stitches as they are seen: Purl 2, *knit 3, purl 2, knit 2, purl 2* repeat from * to * until the end of the row before the edge stitch, knit 3, purl 2.

**Row 48 (Front Side):** Work all the stitches as they are seen: Knit 2, purl 3, *knit 2, purl 2, knit 2, purl 3* repeat from * to * until the end of the row before the edge stitch, knit 2.

**Row 49 (Back Side):** Work all the stitches as they are seen: Purl 2, *knit 3, purl 2, knit 2, purl 2* repeat from * to * until the end of the row before the edge stitch, knit 3, purl 2.

**Row 50 (Front Side):** Work all the stitches as they are seen: Knit 2, purl 3, *knit 2, purl 2, knit 2, purl 3* repeat from * to * until the end of the row before the edge stitch, knit 2.

**Row 51 (Back Side):** Work all the stitches as they are seen: Purl 2, *knit 3, purl 2, knit 2, purl 2* repeat from * to * until the end of the row before the edge stitch, knit 3, purl 2.

**Row 52 (Front Side):** Work all the stitches as they are seen: Knit 2, purl 3, *knit 2, purl 2, knit 2, purl 3* repeat from * to * until the end of the row before the edge stitch, knit 2.

**Row 53 (Back Side):** Work all the stitches as they are seen: Purl 2, *knit 3, purl 2, knit 2, purl 2* repeat from * to * until the end of the row before the edge stitch, knit 3, purl 2.

**Row 54 (Front Side):** Work all the stitches as they are seen: Knit 2, purl 3, *knit 2, purl 2, knit 2, purl 3* repeat from * to * until the end of the row before the edge stitch, knit 2.

**Row 55 (Back Side):** Work all the stitches as they are seen: Purl 2, *knit 3, purl 2, knit 2, purl 2* repeat from * to * until the end of the row before the edge stitch, knit 3, purl 2.

**Row 56 (Front Side):** Work all the stitches as they are seen: Knit 2, purl 3, *knit 2, purl 2, knit 2, purl 3* repeat from * to * until the end of the row before the edge stitch, knit 2.

**Row 57 (Back Side):** Work all the stitches as they are seen: Purl 2, *knit 3, purl 2, knit 2, purl 2* repeat from * to * until the end of the row before the edge stitch, knit 3, purl 2.

**Row 58 (Front Side):** Work all the stitches as they are seen: Knit 2, purl 3, *knit 2, purl 2, knit 2, purl 3* repeat from * to * until the end of the row before the edge stitch, knit 2.

**Row 59 (Back Side):** Work all the stitches as they are seen: Purl 2, *knit 3, purl 2, knit 2, purl 2* repeat from * to * until the end of the row before the edge stitch, knit 3, purl 2.

**Row 60 (Front Side):** Work all the stitches as they are seen: Knit 2, purl 3, *knit 2, purl 2, knit 2, purl 3* repeat from * to * until the end of the row before the edge stitch, knit 2.

**Row 61 (Back Side):** Work all the stitches as they are seen: Purl 2, *knit 3, purl 2, knit 2, purl 2* repeat from * to * until the end of the row before the edge stitch, knit 3, purl 2.

**Row 62 (Front Side):** Work all the stitches as they are seen: Knit 2, purl 3, *knit 2, purl 2, knit 2, purl 3* repeat from * to * until the end of the row before the edge stitch, knit 2.

**Row 63 (Back Side):** Work all the stitches as they are seen: Purl 2, *knit 3, purl 2, knit 2, purl 2* repeat from * to * until the end of the row before the edge stitch, knit 3, purl 2.

**Row 64 (Front Side):** Work all the stitches as they are seen: Knit 2, purl 3, *knit 2, purl 2, knit 2, purl 3* repeat from * to * until the end of the row before the edge stitch, knit 2.

**Row 65 (Back Side):** Work all the stitches as they are seen: Purl 2, *knit 3, purl 2, knit 2, purl 2* repeat from * to * until the end of the row before the edge stitch, knit 3, purl 2.

**Row 66 (Front Side):** Work all the stitches as they are seen: Knit 2, purl 3, *knit 2, purl 2, knit 2, purl 3* repeat from * to * until the end of the row before the edge stitch, knit 2.

**Row 67 (Back Side):** Work all the stitches as they are seen: Purl 2, *knit 3, purl 2, knit 2, purl 2* repeat from * to * until the end of the row before the edge stitch, knit 3, purl 2.

**Row 68 (Front Side):** Work all the stitches as they are seen: Knit 2, purl 3, *knit 2, purl 2, knit 2, purl 3* repeat from * to * until the end of the row before the edge stitch, knit 2.

**Row 69 (Back Side):** Work all the stitches as they are seen: Purl 2, *knit 3, purl 2, knit 2, purl 2* repeat from * to * until the end of the row before the edge stitch, knit 3, purl 2.

**Row 70 (Front Side):** Work all the stitches as they are seen: Knit 2, purl 3, *knit 2, purl 2, knit 2, purl 3* repeat from * to * until the end of the row before the edge stitch, knit 2.

**Row 71 (Back Side):** Work all the stitches as they are seen: Purl 2, *knit 3, purl 2, knit 2, purl 2* repeat from * to * until the end of the row before the edge stitch, knit 3, purl 2.

**Row 72 (Front Side):** Work all the stitches as they are seen: Knit 2, purl 3, *knit 2, purl 2, knit 2, purl 3* repeat from * to * until the end of the row before the edge stitch, knit 2.

**Row 73 (Back Side):** Work all the stitches as they are seen: Purl 2, *knit 3, purl 2, knit 2, purl 2* repeat from * to * until the end of the row before the edge stitch, knit 3, purl 2.

**Row 74 (Front Side):** Work all the stitches as they are seen: Knit 2, purl 3, *knit 2, purl 2, knit 2, purl 3* repeat from * to * until the end of the row before the edge stitch, knit 2.

**Row 75 (Back Side):** Work all the stitches as they are seen: Purl 2, *knit 3, purl 2, knit 2, purl 2* repeat from * to * until the end of the row before the edge stitch, knit 3, purl 2.

**Row 76 (Front Side):** Work all the stitches as they are seen: Knit 2, purl 3, *knit 2, purl 2, knit 2, purl 3* repeat from * to * until the end of the row before the edge stitch, knit 2.

**Row 77 (Back Side):** Work all the stitches as they are seen: Purl 2, *knit 3, purl 2, knit 2, purl 2* repeat from * to * until the end of the row before the edge stitch, knit 3, purl 2.

**Row 78 (Front Side):** Work all the stitches as they are seen: Knit 2, purl 3, *knit 2, purl 2, knit 2, purl 3* repeat from * to * until the end of the row before the edge stitch, knit 2.

**Row 79 (Back Side):** Work all the stitches as they are seen: Purl 2, *knit 3, purl 2, knit 2, purl 2* repeat from * to * until the end of the row before the edge stitch, knit 3, purl 2.

**Row 80 (Front Side):** Work all the stitches as they are seen: Knit 2, purl 3, *knit 2, purl 2, knit 2, purl 3* repeat from * to * until the end of the row before the edge stitch, knit 2.

**Row 81 (Back Side):** Purl 2, *knit 1, slip the next one off the left needle and leave it as is, knit the next 1, purl 2, knit 1, yarn over forward, knit 1, purl 2 * repeat from * to * until the end of the row before the edge stitch, knit 1, slip the next one off the left needle and leave it as is, knit the next 1, purl 2. **Slide down the slipped stitches until the row in which the yarn overs were made.**

**Row 82 (Front Side):** Work all the stitches as they are seen: Knit 2, purl 2, *knit 2, purl 3 (purl yarn over of the previous row), knit 2, purl 2* repeat from * to * until the end of the row before the edge stitch, knit 2.

**Repeat rows:** 3-82.

**Note: Bind off after the last row 41 (or the last row 81). In the last row 41 (or 81), slip the knit stitches off the left needle, following instructions as usual, but do not make yarn overs between 2 knit stitches in this row, in order to avoid holes in the edge row.**

**Bind off as follows:** after the last row 41 (or 81), turn your work over. The Front Side: slip all the stitches from the left needle to the right one; as a result, the working yarn is at the end of the row; turn your work over. The Back Side: slip 2 purlwise from the left needle to the right one, insert the left needle through the 1st slipped stitch, from left to right, and pass it over the 2nd one (now there is 1 stitch on the right needle), *slip 1 purlwise from the left needle to the right one, insert the left needle through the 1st stitch on the right needle, from left to the right, and pass it over the 2nd one (now there is 1 stitch on the right needle)* repeat from * to * until the end of the row.

**Note:** For trimming, bind off loosely, using larger needles than the working ones, as this type of binding off creates a tight chain of small edge stitches that look already finished.

# Pattern 15

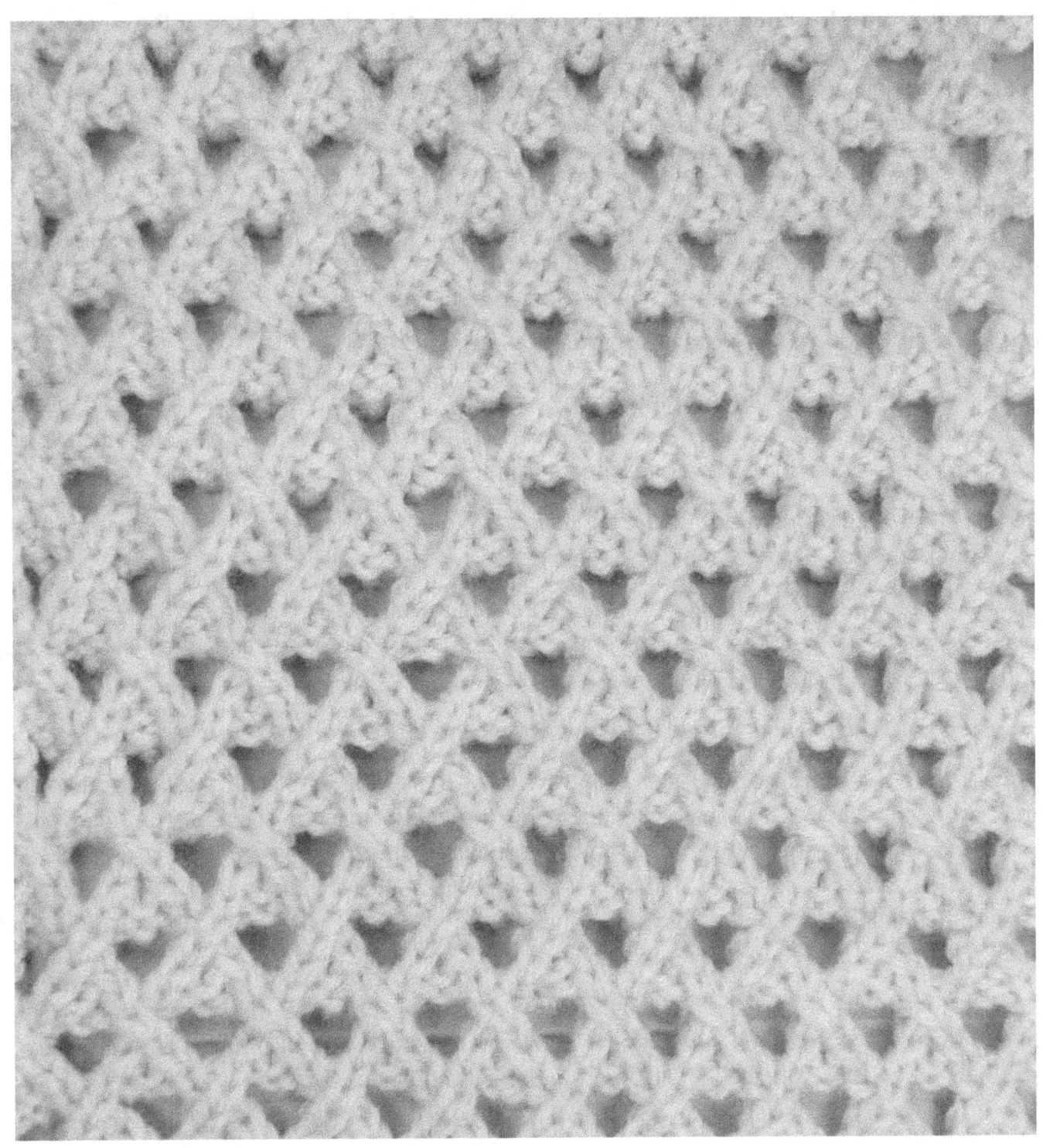

Cast on a multiple of 4, plus 2 edge stitches. Four-stitch repeat. Repeat rows: 1-8. **The edge stitches are not included in the description below and must be added. Slip the first edge stitch, purl the last one.**

**Knit through the front leg, purl as follows:** with the working yarn in front of the stitch, insert the right needle through the stitch from back to front, wrap the working yarn forward (i.e., from yourself) around the tip of the right needle, then pull the working yarn with the right needle through the stitch. The purl stitch that is worked this way sets up the knit stitch to be knitted through the front leg. **Knit tightly.**

**Description:**

**Row 1:** *Purl 1, slip 1 onto a cable needle in front of your work, knit the next 1, then knit the slipped one, purl 1* repeat from * to * until the end of the row.

**Row 2:** *Knit 1, purl 2, knit 1* repeat from * to * until the end of the row.

**Row 3:** *Knit 2 together, yarn over forward (i.e., from yourself) 2 times, knit 2 together as follows: slip 1 onto the right needle knitwise, knit the next 1, then insert the left needle through the slipped stitch and pass it over the knitted one* repeat from * to * until the end of the row.

**Row 4:** *Purl 1, knit 1 (yarn over of the previous row), purl 1 (yarn over of the previous row), purl 1* repeat from * to * until the end of the row.

**Row 5:** Knit 1, *purl 2, slip 1 onto a cable needle behind your work, knit the next 1, then knit the slipped one* repeat from * to * until the end of the row before the edge stitch, the last 3 stitches, purl 2, knit 1.

**Row 6:** *Purl 1, knit 2, purl 1* repeat from * to * until the end of the row.

**Row 7:** Yarn over forward, *knit 2 together as follows: slip the 1st stitch onto the right needle knitwise, knit the next 1, then insert the left needle through the slipped stitch and pass it over the knitted one, knit the next 2 together, yarn over forward 2 times* repeat from * to * until the end of the row before the edge stitch, the last 4 stitches, slip 1 onto the right needle knitwise, knit the next 1, then insert the left needle through the slipped stitch and pass it over the knitted 1, knit the next 2 together, then yarn over forward.

**Row 8:** Knit 1 (yarn over of the previous row), *purl 2, knit 1 (yarn over of the previous row), purl 1 (yarn over of the previous row)* repeat from * to * until the end of the row before the edge stitch, the last 3 stitches, purl 2, knit 1 (yarn over of the previous row).

**Repeat rows:** 1-8.

**Bind off in the last row 1 as follows:** Slip the edge stitch onto the right needle, *purl the next 1 (now there are 2 stitches on the right needle), then insert the left needle through the 1st stitch on the right needle, from left to right, and pass it over the 2nd one (now there is 1 stitch on the right needle), slip 1 onto a cable needle in front of your work, knit the next 1 (now there are 2 stitches on the right needle), then insert the left needle through the 1st stitch on the right needle, from left to right, and pass it over the 2nd one (now there is 1 stitch on the right needle), knit the next 1 that is on the cable needle (now there are 2 stitches on the right needle), then insert the left needle through the 1st stitch on the right needle, from left to right, and pass it over the 2nd one (now there is 1 stitch on the right needle), purl the next 1 (now there are 2 stitches on the right needle), then insert the left needle through the 1st stitch on the right needle, from left to right, and pass it over the 2nd one (now there is 1 stitch on the right needle)* repeat from * to * until the end of the row.

# Pattern 16

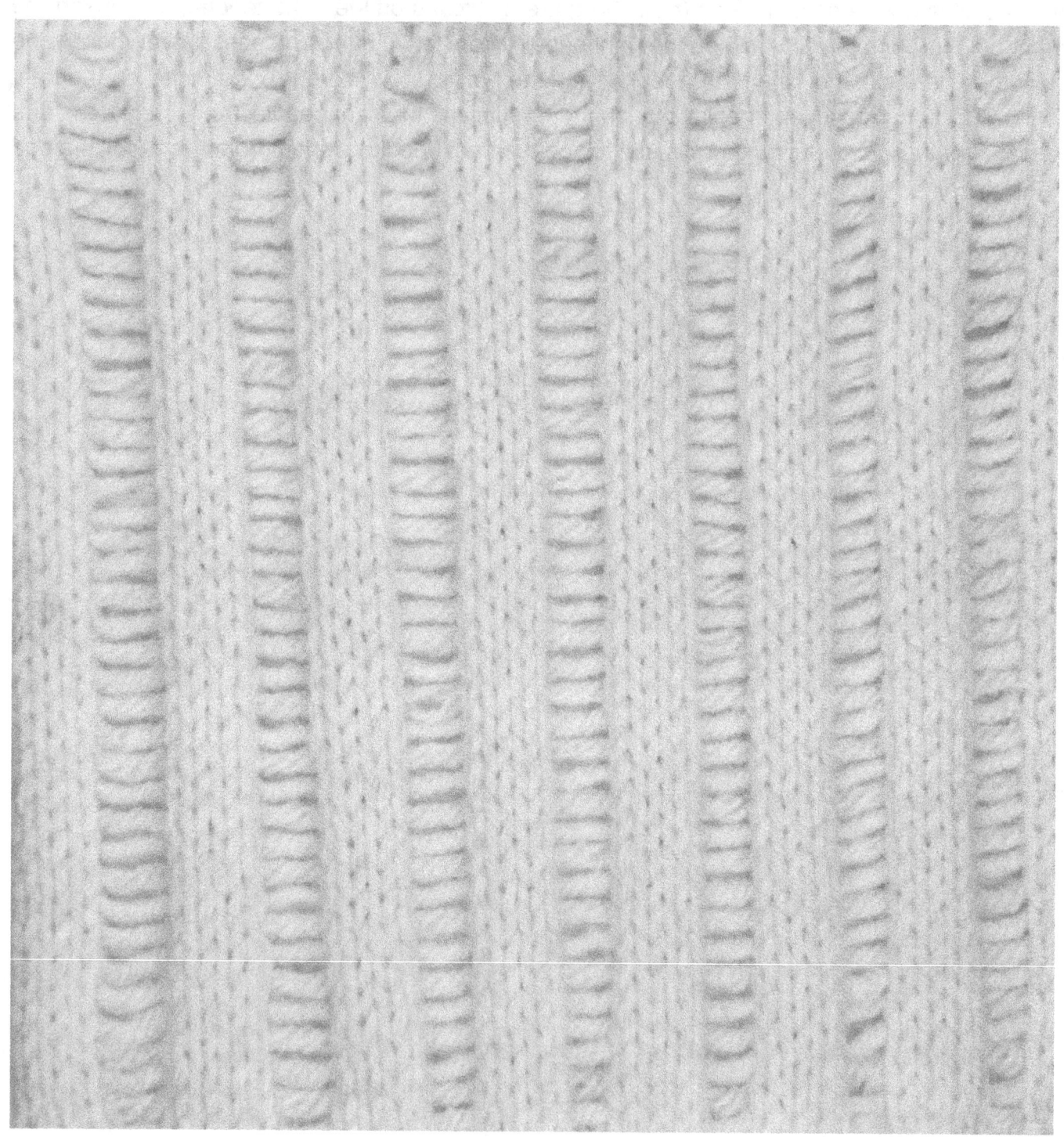

Cast on a multiple of 6, plus 4 for symmetry, and 2 edge stitches. Seven-stitch repeat. Repeat rows: 2-3. **The edge stitches are not included in the description below and must be added. Slip the first edge stitch, purl the last one.**

**Knit through the back leg, purl as follows:** with the working yarn in front of the stitch, insert the right needle through the stitch from back to front, move the working yarn under the right needle and pull it with the needle through the stitch. The purl stitch that is worked this way sets up the knit stitch to be knitted through the back leg.

## Description:

**Row 1 (set up row):** *Knit 4, purl 1, yarn over forward (i.e., from yourself), purl 1* repeat from * to * until the end of the row before the edge stitch, knit 4.

**Row 2:** *Purl 4, knit 1, purl 1, knit 1* repeat from * to * until the end of the row before the edge stitch, purl 4.

**Row 3:** *Knit 4, purl 1, knit 1, purl 1* repeat from * to * until the end of the row before the edge stitch knit 4.

**Repeat rows:** 2-3.

**Bind off after the last row 2 as follows:** Bind off knit 4, purl 1, slip 1 off the left needle and leave it as is, *bind off purl 1, knit 4, purl 1, then slip the next 1 off the left needle and leave it as is* repeat from * to * until the end of the row before the edge stitch, bind off purl 1, knit 4. **Note: Now slide down all the slipped stitches, from top to bottom, until the 1st row.**

# Pattern 17

Cast on a multiple of 7, plus 5 for symmetry, plus 2 edge stitches. Eight-stitch repeat. Repeat rows: 2-3. **The edge stitches are not included in the description below and must be added. Slip the first edge stitch, purl the last one.**

**Knit through the back leg, purl as follows:** with the working yarn in front of the stitch, insert the right needle through the stitch from back to front, move the working yarn under the right needle and pull it with the needle through the stitch. The purl stitch that is worked this way sets up the knit stitch to be knitted through the back leg.

# Description:

**Row 1 (set up row):** *Knit 5, purl 1, yarn over forward (i.e., from yourself), purl 1* repeat from * to * until the end of the row before the edge stitch, knit 5.

**Row 2:** *Purl 5, knit 1, purl 1, knit 1* repeat from * to * until the end of the row before the edge stitch, purl 5.

**Row 3:** *Knit 5, purl 1, knit 1, purl 1* repeat from * to * until the end of the row before the edge stitch knit 5.

**Repeat rows:** 2-3.

**Bind off after the last row 2 as follows:** Bind off knit 5, purl 1, slip 1 off the left needle and leave it as is, *bind off purl 1, knit 5, purl 1, slip the next 1 off the left needle and leave it as is* repeat from * to * until the end of the row before the edge stitch, bind off purl 1, knit 5. **Note: Now slide down all the slipped stitches, from top to bottom, until the 1st row.**

# Pattern 18

Cast on a multiple of 17, using regular way of casting on stitches, plus 16 for symmetry, and 2 edge stitches. Eighteen-stitch repeat. Repeat rows: 1-10. **The edge stitches are not included in the description below and must be added. Slip the first edge stitch, purl the last one.**

**Knit through the back leg, purl as follows:** with the working yarn in front of the stitch, insert the right needle through the stitch from back to front, move the working yarn under the right needle and pull it with the needle through the stitch. The purl stitch that is worked this way sets up the knit stitch to be knitted through the back leg.

## Description:

**Row 1:** *Slip 8 behind your work, knit the next 8, then knit the slipped 8, purl 1, yarn over forward (i.e., from yourself)* repeat from * to * until the end of the row before the edge stitch, the last 16 stitches, slip 8 behind your work, knit the next 8, then knit the slipped 8.

**Row 2:** *Purl 16, knit 2* repeat from * to * until the end of the row before the edge stitch, purl the last 16.

**Row 3:** *Knit 16, purl 2* repeat from * to * until the end of the row before the edge stitch, knit the last 16.

**Row 4:** *Purl 16, knit 2* repeat from * to * until the end of the row before the edge stitch, purl the last 16.

**Row 5:** *Knit 16, purl 2 * repeat from * to * until the end of the row before the edge stitch, knit the last 16.

**Row 6:** *Purl 16, knit 2* repeat from * to * until the end of the row before the edge stitch, purl the last 16.

**Row 7:** *Knit 16, purl 2* repeat from * to * until the end of the row before the edge stitch, knit the last 16.

**Row 8:** *Purl 16, knit 2* repeat from * to * until the end of the row before the edge stitch, purl the last 16.

**Row 9:** *Knit 16, purl 2* repeat from * to * until the end of the row before the edge stitch, knit the last 16.

**Row 10:** *Purl 16, knit 2* repeat from * to * until the end of the row before the edge stitch, purl the last 16.

**Repeat rows:** 1-10.

**Note: After the last row 10, work the next row before binding off as follows:**

*Slip 8 behind your work, knit the next 8, then knit the slipped 8, slip the next 2 purl stitches off the left needle and leave them as they are, then make 6 new stitches to enlarge the space between the braids in the edge row* repeat from * to * until the end of the row before the edge stitch, the last 16 stitches, slip 8 behind your work, knit the next 8, then knit the slipped 8.

**Bind off as follows:** After the last row, turn your work over. The Back Side: slip all the stitches from the left needle to the right one (as a result, the working yarn is at the end of the right needle); turn your work over. The Front Side: slip 2 purlwise from the left needle to the right one, insert the left needle through the 1$^{st}$ slipped stitch, from left to right, and pass it over the 2$^{nd}$ one (now there is 1 stitch on the right needle), *slip 1 purlwise from the left needle to the right one, insert the left needle through the 1$^{st}$ stitch on the right needle, from left to the right, and pass it over the 2$^{nd}$ one (now there is 1 stitch on the right needle)* repeat from * to * until the end of the row.

**Note:** For trimming, bind off loosely, using larger needles than the working ones, as this type of binding off creates a tight chain of small edge stitches.

# Pattern 19

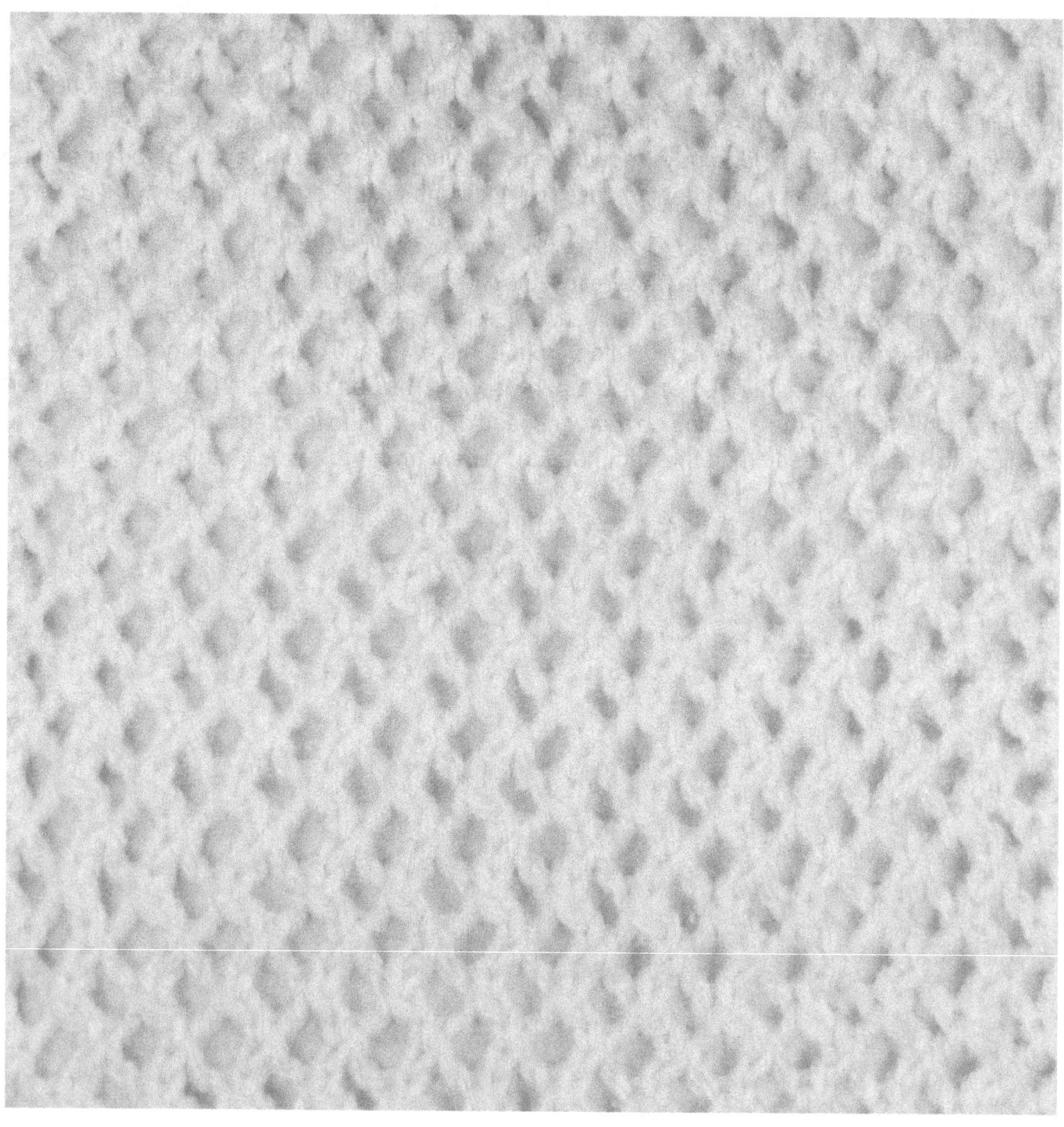

Cast on a multiple of 2, plus 2 edge stitches. Two-stitch repeat. Repeat rows: 1-4.

**The edge stitches are not included in the description below and must be added. Slip the first stitch; purl the last stitch as in knitting through the back leg as follows:** with the working yarn in front of the stitch, insert the right needle through the stitch from back to front, move the working yarn under the right needle and pull it with the needle through the stitch. **Knit tightly.**

# Description:

**Row 1:** *Knit 2 together through the front legs, yarn over forward (i.e., from yourself)* repeat from * to * until the end of the row.

**Row 2:** Purl all the stitches as if to purl in knitting through the back leg as follows: with the working yarn in front of the stitch, insert the right needle through the stitch from back to front, move the working yarn under the right needle and pull it with the needle through the stitch. The purl stitch that is worked this way sets up the knit stitch to be knitted through the back leg.

**Row 3:** *Yarn over forward, knit 2 together through the back legs* repeat from * to * until the end of the row.

**Row 4:** Purl all the stitches as if to purl in knitting through the front leg as follows: with the working yarn in front of the stitch, insert the right needle through the stitch from back to front, wrap the working yarn forward (i.e., from yourself) around the tip of the right needle, then pull the working yarn with the right needle through the stitch. The purl stitch that is worked this way sets up the knit stitch to be knitted through the front leg.

**Repeat rows:** 1-4.

**Bind off after the last row 4 as follows:** Slip the edge stitch onto the right needle, knit the next 1 through the front leg, insert the left needle through the slipped edge stitch, from left to right, and pass it over the knitted stitch, *now there is 1 stitch on the right needle, knit the next 1 through the front leg (now there are 2 stitches on the right needle), insert the left needle through the 1st stitch on the right needle, from left to right, and pass it over the 2nd one* repeat from * to * until the end of the row.

# Pattern 20

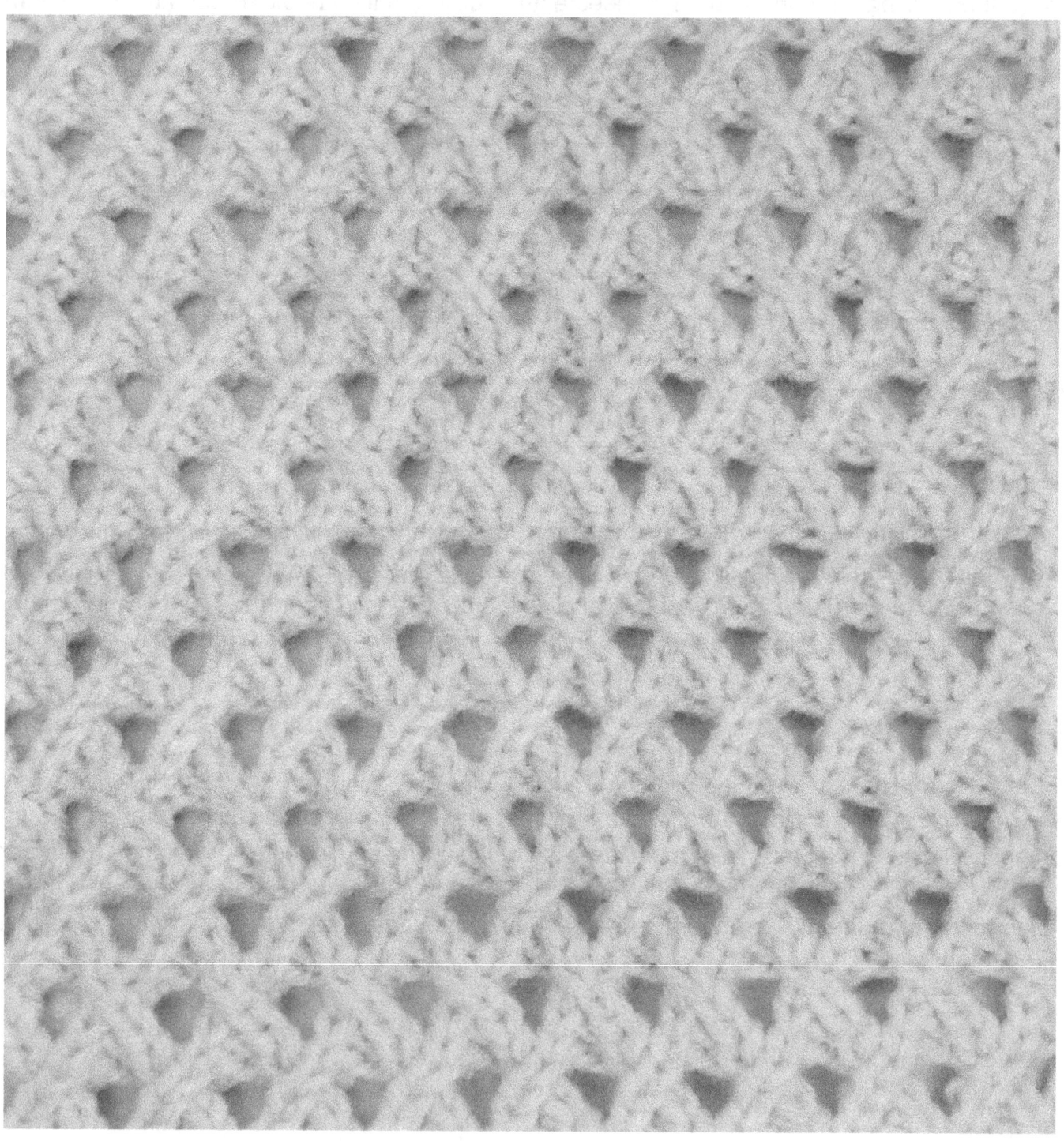

Cast on a multiple of 4, plus 2 edge stitches. Four-stitch repeat. Repeat rows: 1-8.

**The edge stitches are not included in the description below and must be added. Slip the first edge stitch, purl the last one.**

**Knit through the back leg, purl as follows:** with the working yarn in front of the stitch, insert the right needle through the stitch from back to front, move the working yarn under the right needle and pull it with the needle through the stitch. The purl stitch that is worked this way sets up the knit stitch to be knitted through the back leg.

# Description:

**Row 1:** *Purl 1, slip 1 onto a cable needle in front of your work, knit the next 1, then knit the slipped 1, purl 1* repeat from * to * until the end of the row.

**Row 2:** *Knit 1, purl 2, knit 1* repeat from * to * until the end of the row.

**Row 3:** *Knit 2 together through the front legs as follows: slip 1 purlwise, then insert the right needle through the back leg of the next stitch from back to front and slip it onto the right needle, then return both stitches onto the left needle, now knit 2 together through the front legs, then yarn over forward (i.e., from yourself) 2 times, knit 2 together through the back legs* repeat from * to * until the end of the row.

**Row 4:** *Purl 1, purl 1 (yarn over of the previous row), knit 1 (yarn over of the previous row), purl 1* repeat from * to * until the end of the row.

**Row 5:** Knit 1, *purl 2, slip 1 onto a cable needle behind your work, knit the next 1, then knit the slipped one* repeat from * to * until the end of the row before the edge stitch, purl 2, knit 1.

**Row 6:** *Purl 1, knit 2, purl 1* repeat from * to * until the end of the row.

**Row 7:** Yarn over forward, *knit 2 together through the back legs, knit the next 2 together through the front legs as follows: slip 1 purlwise, then insert the right needle through the back leg of the next stitch, from back to front, and slip it onto the right needle, then return both stitches onto the left needle, now knit 2 together through the front legs, then yarn over forward 2 times* repeat from * to * until the end of the row before the edge stitch, the last 4 stitches, knit 2 together through the back legs, knit the next 2 together through the front legs as follows: slip 1 purlwise, then insert the right needle through the back leg of the next stitch, from back to front, and slip it onto the right needle, then return both stitches onto the left needle, now knit 2 together through the front legs, then yarn over forward.

**Row 8:** Knit 1 (yarn over of the previous row), *purl 2, purl 1 (yarn over of the previous row), knit 1 (yarn over of the previous row)* repeat from * to * until the end of the row before the edge stitch, the last 3 stitches, purl 2, knit 1 (yarn over of the previous row).

**Repeat rows:** 1-8.

**Bind off in the last row 1 as follows:** Slip the edge stitch onto the right needle, *purl the next 1 (now there are 2 stitches on the right needle), then insert the left needle through the 1st stitch on the right needle, from left to right, and pass it over the 2nd one (now there is 1 stitch on the right needle), slip 1 onto a cable needle in front of your work, knit the next 1 (now there are 2 stitches on the right needle), then insert the left needle through the 1st stitch on the right needle, from left to right, and pass it over the 2nd one (now there is 1 stitch on the right needle), knit the next 1 that is on the cable needle (now there are 2 stitches on the right needle), then insert the left needle through the 1st stitch on the right needle, from left to right, and pass it over the 2nd one (now there is 1 stitch on the right needle), purl the next 1 (now there are 2 stitches on the right needle), then insert the left needle through the 1st stitch on the right needle, from left to right, and pass it over the 2nd one (now there is 1 stitch on the right needle)* repeat from * to * until the end of the row.

# Pattern 21
## Option 1

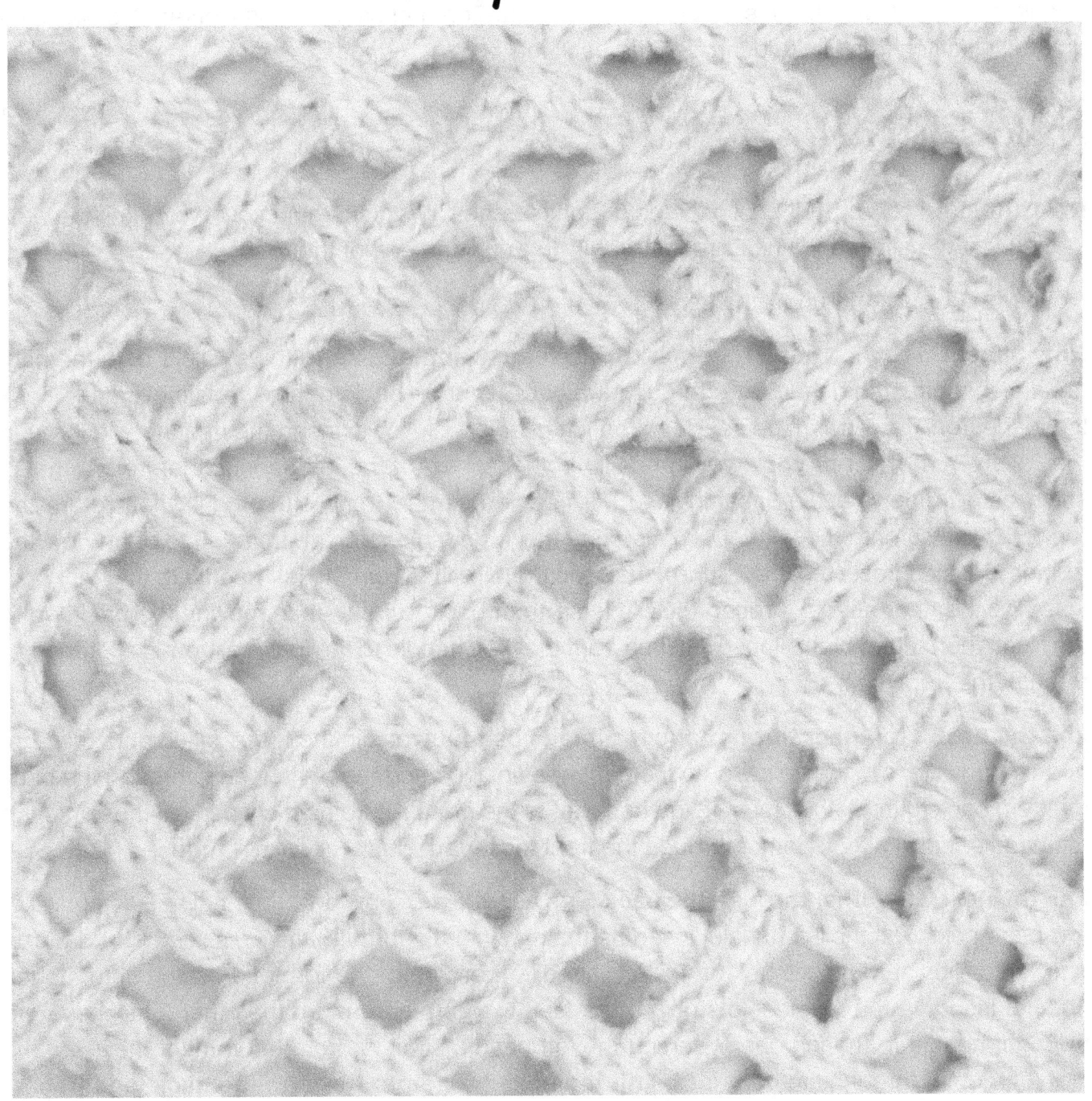

Cast on a multiple of 8, plus 2 edge stitches. Eight-stitch repeat. Repeat rows: **5-12. The edge stitches are not included in the description below and must be added. Slip the first edge stitch, purl the last one. Needles: U.S. no. 8 (5 mm).**

**Knit through the back leg, purl as follows:** with the working yarn in front of the stitch, insert the right needle through the stitch from back to front, move the working yarn under the right needle and pull it with the needle through the stitch. The purl stitch that is worked this way sets up the knit stitch to be knitted through the back leg.

# *Description:*

**Row 1 (set up row):** *Knit 2, slip the next 2 onto a cable needle behind your work, knit the next 2, then knit the slipped 2, knit 2* repeat from * to * until the end of the row.

**Row 2 (set up row):** Purl all the stitches.

**Row 3 (set up row):** *Knit 2 together through the front legs as follows**: slip 1 onto the right needle, inserting the right needle through the back leg from back to front, thus moving the back leg to the front; then swap the next 2 on the left needle as follows: insert the right needle through the 2$^{nd}$ stitch **in front of your work** and slip both stitches off the left needle, then return the 1$^{st}$ stitch onto the left needle, inserting the left needle straight, from left to right, then return the former 2$^{nd}$ stitch onto the left needle, inserting the left needle straight, from left to right (now the former 2$^{nd}$ stitch becomes the 1$^{st}$ one), then slip the 1$^{st}$ stitch from the left needle to the right one, inserting the right needle through the back leg from back to front, thus moving the back leg to the front, then return both slipped stitches from the right needle to the left one, now knit 2 together through the front legs;

**knit the next 2 together through the front legs as follows**: slip the first 1 stitch onto the right needle purlwise, slip the next 1 onto the right needle, inserting the right needle through the back leg from back to front, thus moving the back leg to the front, return both slipped stitches onto the left needle, now knit 2 together through the front legs; **yarn over forward 4 times**;

**knit the next 2 together through the back legs as follows**: slip 1 onto the right needle purlwise, swap the next 2 on the left needle, inserting the right needle through the 2$^{nd}$ stitch **behind** the 1$^{st}$ one, thus slipping both stitches off the left needle, then return the former 1$^{st}$ stitch onto the left needle, inserting the left needle straight, from left to right, then return the other 2 stitches from the right needle to the left one, inserting the left needle straight, from left to right, now knit the first 2 together through the back legs; **knit the next 2 together through the back legs*** repeat from * to * until the end of the row.

**Row 4 (set up row):** *Purl 2, work the next 4 (yarn overs of the previous row) as follows: knit 1 through the front leg, purl 1, knit 1 through the front leg, purl 1, then purl 2* repeat from * to * until the end of the row.

**Row 5:** Knit 2, *knit 1 through the back leg, knit 1 through the front leg, knit 1 through the back leg, knit 1 through the front leg, then slip 2 onto a cable needle **in front of your work**, knit the next 2, then knit the slipped 2* repeat from * to * until the end of the row before the edge stitch, the last 6 stitches, knit 1 through the back

leg, knit 1 through the front leg, knit 1 through the back leg, knit 1 through the front leg, then knit the last 2.

**Row 6:** Purl all the stitches.

**Row 7:** *** Yarn over forward 2 times, knit 3 together through the back legs as follows**: slip 1 purlwise onto the right needle, inserting the right needle from right to left; swap the next 2 on the left needle as follows: insert the right needle through the 2$^{nd}$ stitch **behind the 1$^{st}$ stitch** and slip both stitches off the left needle, then pick up the 1$^{st}$ stitch onto the left needle, inserting the left needle straight, from left to right (now the 2$^{nd}$ stitch is on the right needle, and the 1$^{st}$ one is on the left needle), then take an extra needle and pick up the edge stitch that is **3 rows below the 2$^{nd}$ stitch on the left needle**, inserting the extra needle through this edge stitch **behind your work from bottom to top**, then move it onto the right needle, inserting the right needle straight, from right to left; then move these 3 slipped stitches from the right needle to the left one and knit them together through the back legs; **knit 3 together through the back legs as follows**: slip 1 purlwise from the left needle to the right one; slip the next 1 from the left needle to the right one, **inserting the right needle from back to front**, thus moving the back leg to the front; then take an extra needle and pick up the edge stitch **3 rows below the 1$^{st}$ stitch on the left needle**, inserting the extra needle through this edge stitch **behind your work from bottom to top**; then move this edge stitch onto the right needle, inserting the right needle through this stitch straight, from right to left; then move these 3 slipped stitches from the right needle to the left one, then knit them together through the back legs; **knit 3 together through the front legs as follows:** take an extra needle and pick up the edge stitch **3 rows below the 1$^{st}$ stitch on the left needle**, **inserting the extra needle behind your work from bottom to top**, and then move it onto the right needle, **inserting the right needle through this edge stitch from back to front, thus moving the back leg to the front**; then slip the next 1 onto the right needle, inserting the right needle through this stitch from back to front, thus moving the back leg to the front; then swap the next 2 on the left needle as follows: insert the right needle through the 2$^{nd}$ stitch **in front of your work** and slip both stitches off the left needle, then pick up the 1$^{st}$ stitch onto the left needle, inserting the left needle straight, from left to right, then return the 2$^{nd}$ stitch onto the left needle, inserting the left needle straight (now the former 2$^{nd}$ stitch becomes the 1$^{st}$ one), then slip the 1$^{st}$ stitch onto the right needle, inserting the right needle through this stitch from back to front, thus moving the back leg to the front, then move these 3 slipped stitches from the right needle to the left one and knit them together through the front legs;

**knit 3 together through the front legs as follows:** take an extra needle and pick up the edge stitch **3 rows below the 1st stitch** on the left needle, inserting the extra needle **behind your work from bottom to top**, then slip this edge stitch onto the right needle, **inserting the right needle through this stitch from back to front**, thus moving the back leg to the front; then slip the next stitch from the left needle to the right one, inserting the right needle from back to front, thus moving the back leg to the front; then slip the next 1 from the left needle to the right one, inserting the right needle from back to front; then return these 3 slipped stitches onto the left needle and knit them together through the front legs; then **yarn over forward 2 times\*** repeat from \* to \* until the end of the row.

**Row 8:** \*Knit 1 through the front leg (yarn over of the previous row), purl 1 (yarn over of the previous row), purl

4, knit 1 through the front leg (yarn over of the previous row), purl 1 (yarn over of the previous row)\* repeat from \* to \* until the end of the row.

**Row 9:** \*Knit 1 through the back leg, knit 1 through the front leg, slip the next 2 onto a cable needle **behind your work**, knit the next 2, then knit the slipped 2, knit the next 1 through the back leg, knit the next 1 through the front leg\* repeat from \* to \* until the end of the row.

**Row 10:** Purl all the stitches.

**Row 11: Knit 3 together through the front legs as follows**: take an extra needle and insert it **behind your work through the edge stitch 3 rows below the 1st stitch on the left needle, inserting the extra needle through the edge stitch from bottom to top**, and slip it onto the right needle, inserting the right needle through this edge stitch from back to front, thus moving the back leg to the front; slip the next 1 onto the right needle, inserting the right needle through the stitch from back to front, thus moving the back leg to the front; then swap the next 2 on the left needle as follows: insert the right needle through the 2nd stitch **in front of your work** and slip both stitches off the left needle, then return the 1st stitch onto the left needle, inserting the left needle straight, from left to right, then return the 2nd stitch onto the left needle, inserting the left needle straight (thus the former 2nd stitch becomes the 1st one), then slip the 1st stitch from the left needle to the right one, inserting the right needle from back to front, thus moving the back leg to the front, then return these 3 slipped stitches onto the left needle and knit them together through the front legs;

**knit the next 3 together as follows:** take an extra needle and insert it **behind** your work through the edge stitch **3 rows below the 1st stitch on the left needle, inserting this extra needle from bottom to top**, and slip it onto the right needle, inserting the right needle through this edge stitch from back to front, thus moving the back leg to the front; then slip the next 1 onto the right needle, inserting the right needle through the stitch straight, from right to left, then slip the next 1 onto the right needle, inserting the right needle through the stitch from back to front, thus moving the back leg to the front, then return these 3 stitches from the right needle onto the left one and knit them together through the front legs;

*****yarn over forward 4 times**; then **knit 3 together through the back legs as follows:** insert the right needle through the 1st stitch on the left needle purlwise and slip it onto the right needle; then swap the next 2 on the left needle as follows: insert the right needle through the 2nd stitch **behind** your work and slip both stitches off the left needle, then pick up the 1st stitch onto the left needle, inserting it straight, from left to right (now the former 2nd stitch is on the right needle, and the former 1st stitch is on the left needle), then take an extra needle and insert it **behind your work from bottom to top** through the edge stitch **3 rows below the 2nd stitch on the left needle** and slip it straight onto the right needle, inserting the right needle from right to left, then return 3 slipped stitches from the right needle to the left one and knit them together through the back legs;

**knit the next 3 together through the back legs as follows:** slip 1 purlwise from the left needle to the right one, slip the next 1 from the left needle to the right one, inserting the right needle through the stitch from back to front, thus moving the back leg to the front, then take an extra needle, insert it **behind your work from bottom to top through the edge stitch 3 rows below the 1st stitch on the left needle** and slip it onto the right needle, inserting the right needle through this stitch straight, from right to left, then return these 3 stitches onto the left needle and knit them together through the back legs;

**knit the next 3 together as follows:** take an extra needle and pick up the edge stitch **3 rows below the 1st stitch on the left needle, inserting the extra needle behind your work from bottom to top**, then slip it onto the right needle, **inserting the right needle through this edge stitch from back to front**, thus moving the back leg of this edge stitch to the front; then slip the next 1 from the left needle to the right one, inserting the right needle through the stitch from back to front, thus moving the back leg to the front; then **swap the next 2 on the left needle as follows:** insert the right needle through the 2nd stitch **in front of your work** and slip both stitches off the left needle, then pick up the former 1st stitch onto the left needle, inserting the left needle straight, from left to right, then return the former 2nd stitch onto the left needle, inserting the left needle straight, from left to right (thus the former 2nd stitch becomes the 1st one), then slip the 1st stitch onto the right needle, inserting the right needle through this stitch from back to front, thus moving the back leg to the front, then move these 3 slipped stitches from the right needle to the left one and knit them together through the front legs; **knit the next 3 together through the front legs as follows:** take an extra needle and pick up the edge stitch **3 rows below the 2nd stitch on the left needle**, inserting the extra needle **behind your work from bottom to top**, then slip it onto the right needle, **inserting the right needle through this edge stitch from back to front**, thus moving the back leg to the front; then slip the next 1 from the left needle to the right one, inserting the right needle through the stitch from back to front, thus moving the back leg to the front; then slip the next 1 from the left needle to the right one, inserting the right needle through the stitch from back to front, thus moving the back leg to the front; then return these 3 slipped stitches from the right needle to the left one and knit them together through the front legs* repeat from * to * until the last 4 stitches before the edge stitch, then **yarn over forward 4 times, knit the next 3 together through the back legs as follows:** slip 1 purlwise from the left needle to the right one, then take an extra needle and pick up the edge stitch **3 rows below the 2nd stitch on the left needle**, inserting the extra needle **behind your work from bottom to top**, then slip it onto the right needle, inserting the right needle straight, from right to left; swap the next 2 on the left needle as follows: insert the right needle through the 2nd stitch **behind** your work and slip both stitches off the left needle, then return the former 1st stitch onto the left needle, inserting the left needle straight, from left to right, then move 3 slipped stitches from the right needle to the left one and knit them together through the back legs; then

**knit the last 3 together through the back legs as follows:** slip the 1st stitch from the left needle to the right one, inserting the right needle through the stitch straight, from right to left, then slip the next 1 from the left needle to the right one, inserting the right needle straight, from right to left; then take an extra needle, insert it **behind your work from bottom to top through the edge stitch 3 rows below the last slipped stitch** and slip it onto the right needle, inserting the right needle through this edge stitch straight, from right to left, then move these 3 slipped stitches from the right needle to the left one and knit them together through the back legs.

**Row 12:** *Purl 2, work the next 4 (yarn overs of the previous row) as follows: knit 1 through the front leg, purl 1, knit 1 through the front leg, purl 1, then purl 2* repeat from * to * until the end of the row.

**Repeat rows: 5-12.**

**Bind off in the last row 11 (note: without yarn overs) as follows:** Slip the edge stitch onto the right needle, knit the next 3 together as described in row 11, then insert the left needle through the slipped edge stitch, from left to right, and pass it over the received stitch after knitting 3 together (now there is 1 stitch on the right needle), *knit the next 3 together as described in row 11, then insert the left needle through the stitch that is on the right needle, from left to right, and pass it over the received stitch after knitting 3 together (now there is 1 stitch on the right needle)* repeat from * to * until the end of the row.

# Option 2

Knit the same as option 1 using needles U.S. no. 10 ½ (6.5 mm). Knit tightly.

# Pattern 22

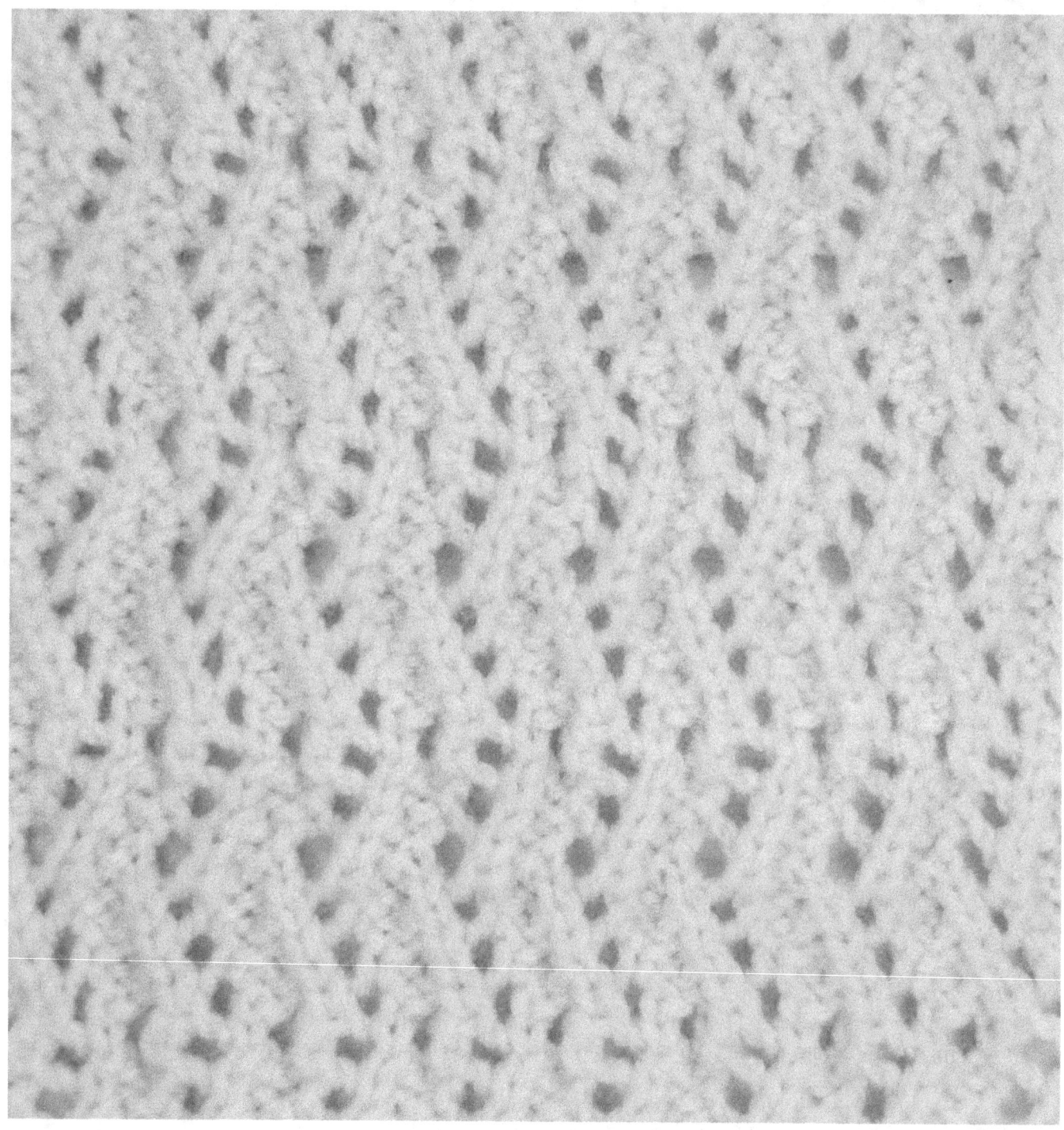

Cast on a multiple of 4, plus 1, plus 2 edge stitches. Four-stitch repeat. Repeat rows: 1-12. **The edge stitches are not included in the description below and must be added. Slip the first**

**edge stitch, purl the last one as in knitting through the back leg as follows:** with the working yarn in front of the stitch, insert the right needle through the stitch from back to front, move the working yarn under the right needle and pull it with the needle through the stitch.

**Knit through the front leg, purl as follows:** with the working yarn in front of the stitch, insert the right needle through the stitch from back to front, wrap the working yarn forward (i.e., from yourself) around the tip of the right needle, then pull the working yarn with the right needle through the stitch. The purl stitch that is worked this way sets up the knit stitch to be knitted through the front leg.

# Description:

**Row 1:** Purl 1, *purl 1, knit 2 together, yarn over forward (i.e., from yourself), purl 1* repeat from * to * until the end of the row.

**Row 2:** *Knit 1, purl 2, knit 1* repeat from * to * until the end of the row before the edge stitch, knit 1.

**Row 3:** Purl 1, *knit 2 together, yarn over forward, purl 2* repeat from * to * until the end of the row.

**Row 4:** *Knit 2, purl 2* repeat from * to * until the end of the row before the edge stitch, knit 1.

**Row 5:** Knit 2 together, *yarn over forward, purl 2, knit 2 together* repeat from * to * until the end of the row before the edge stitch, yarn over forward, purl 3.

**Row 6:** Purl 1, *yarn over forward, knit 2 together through the back legs as follows: slip the 1st stitch onto the right needle, inserting the right needle through the stitch from front to back, thus moving the front leg to the back, slip the 2nd stitch onto the right needle the same way, then return both stitches onto the left needle, now knit 2 together through the back legs, purl 2* repeat from * to * until the end of the row.

**Row 7:** Purl 1, *yarn over forward, knit 2 together through the back legs as described in row 6, purl 2* repeat from * to * until the end of the row.

**Row 8:** *Knit 2, purl 2* repeat from * to * until the end of the row before the edge stitch, knit 1.

**Row 9:** Purl 1, *purl 1, yarn over forward, knit 2 together through the back legs as described in row 6, purl 1* repeat from * to * until the end of the row.

**Row 10:** *Knit 1, purl 2, knit 1* repeat from * to * until the end of the row before the edge stitch, knit 1.

**Row 11:** Purl 1, *purl 2, yarn over forward, knit 2 together through the back legs as described in row 6* repeat from * to * until the end of the row.

**Row 12:** *Purl 2, knit 2* repeat from * to * until the end of the row before the edge stitch, knit 1.

**Repeat rows: 1-12.**

**Bind off in the last row 8 as follows:** Slip the edge stitch onto the right needle, knit the next 1 through the front leg, insert the left needle through the slipped edge stitch, from left to right, and pass it over the knitted stitch, *now there is 1 stitch on the right needle, knit the next 1 through the front leg (now there are 2 stitches on the right needle), insert the left needle through the 1st stitch on the right needle, from left to right, and pass it over the 2nd one* repeat from * to * until the end of the row.

# Pattern 23

## Reversible

Cast on a multiple of 12, plus 6 for symmetry, and plus 2 edge stitches. Twelve-stitch repeat. Repeat rows: 3-10. **The edge stitches are not included in the description below and must be added. Slip the first edge stitch; purl the last one as in knitting through the back legs as follows:** with the working yarn in front of the stitch, insert the right needle through the stitch from back to front, move the working yarn under the right needle and pull it with the needle through the stitch. **Note: Knit tightly, especially the stitches adjacent to the holes.**

## Description:

**Row 1 (set up row, Front Side):** Knit all the stitches.

**Row 2 (set up row, Back Side):** Knit all the stitches.

**Row 3 (Front Side):** *Knit 5 through the front legs, knit 1 through the back leg, bind off the next 6 through the back legs, binding off the 1st stitch tightly, as follows: knit 2 together through the back legs, slip 1 from the right needle to the left one, knit the next 2 together, slip 1 from the right needle to the left one, knit the next 2 together, slip 1 from the right needle to the left one, knit the next 2 together, slip 1 from the right needle to the left one, knit the next 2 together, slip 1 from the right needle to the left one, knit the next 2 together, slip 1 from the right needle to the left one, (**note**: count the last stitch as the 1st of the next 5 stitches)* repeat from * to * until the end of the row before the edge stitch, the last 6 stitches, knit 5 through the front legs, knit 1 through the back leg.

**Row 4 (Back Side):** Knit 5 through the front legs, knit 1 through the back leg, *make 6 new stitches on the right needle as follows: move the working yarn on top of the left needle, then insert the right needle through the backside of this loop from back to front and slip this loop onto the right needle, repeat 5 more times, then knit 1 through the back leg tightly, knit 4 through the front legs, knit 1 through the back leg* repeat from * to * until the end of the row.

**Row 5 (Front Side):** Knit 5 through the front legs, knit 1 through the back leg, *knit 6 through the back legs, then knit the next 1 through the back leg tightly, knit 4 through the front legs, knit 1 through the back leg* repeat from * to * until the end of the row.

**Row 6 (Back Side):** Knit all the stitches through the front legs.

**Row 7 (Front Side):** *Bind off 6 through the back legs, binding off the 1st stitch tightly, as follows: knit 2 together through the back legs, slip 1 from the right needle to the left one, knit the next 2 together, slip 1 from the right needle to the left one, knit the next 2 together, slip 1 from the right needle to the left one, knit the next 2 together, slip 1 from the right needle to the left one, knit the next 2 together, slip 1 from the right needle to the left one, knit the next 2 together, slip 1 from the right needle to the left one (**note:** count the last stitch as the 1st of the next 5 stitches), knit 5 through the front legs, knit 1 through the back leg* repeat from * to * until the end of the row before the edge stitch, bind off the last 6 as described above in this row.

**Row 8 (Back Side):** *Make 6 new stitches on the right needle as follows: move the working yarn on top of the left needle, then insert the right needle through the backside of this loop from back to front and slip this loop onto the right needle, repeat 5 more times, knit 1 through the back leg tightly, knit 4 through the front legs, knit 1 through the back leg* repeat from * to * until the end of the row before the edge stitch, make 6 new stitches on the right needle as described above in this row.

**Row 9 (Front Side):** *Knit 6 through the back legs, knit 1 through the back leg tightly, knit 4 through the front legs, knit 1 through the back leg* repeat from * to * before the edge stitch, knit the last 6 through the back legs.

**Row 10 (Back Side):** Knit all the stitches through the front legs.

**Repeat rows:** 3-10.

**Bind off after the last row 10 as follows:** Slip the edge stitch onto the right needle, knit the next 1 through the front leg, insert the left needle through the slipped edge stitch, from left to right, and pass it over the knitted stitch, *now there is 1 stitch on the right needle, knit the next 1 through the front leg (now there are 2 stitches on the right needle), insert the left needle through the 1st stitch on the right needle, from left to right, and pass it over the 2nd one* repeat from * to * until the end of the row.

# Pattern 24

## Reversible

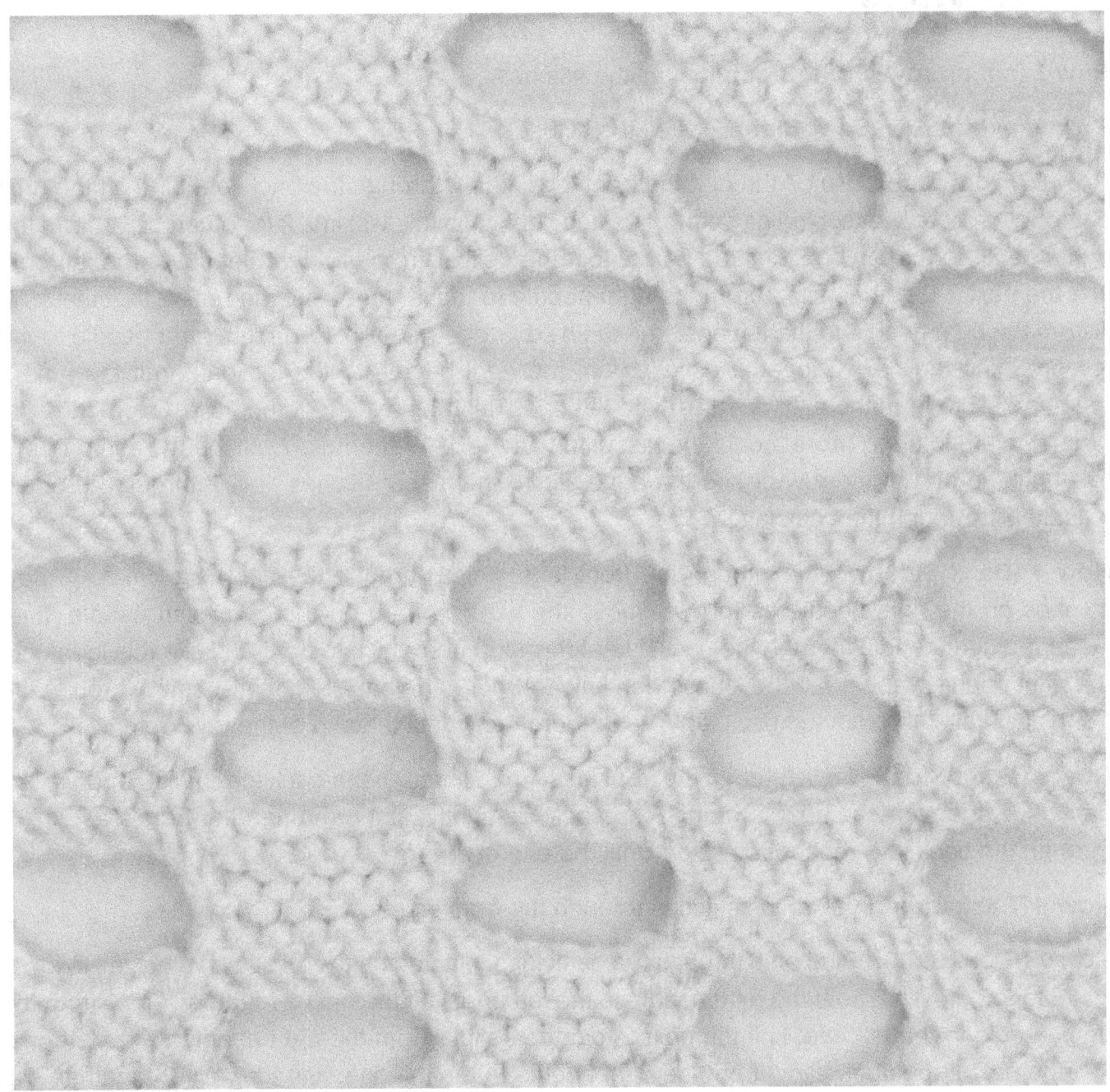

Cast on a multiple of 16, plus 8 for symmetry, and plus 2 edge stitches. Sixteen-stitch repeat. Repeat rows: 3-10. **The edge stitches are not included in the description below and must**

**be added. Slip the first edge stitch, purl the last one in knitting through the back leg as follows:** with the working yarn in front of the stitch, insert the right needle through the stitch from back to front, move the working yarn under the right needle and pull it with the needle through the stitch. **Note: Knit tightly, especially the stitches adjacent to the holes.**

# Description:

**Row 1 (set up row, Front Side):** Knit all the stitches.

**Row 2 (set up row, Back Side):** Knit all the stitches.

**Row 3 (Front Side):** *Knit 7 through the front legs, knit 1 through the back leg, bind off the next 8 through the back legs, binding off the 1st stitch tightly, as follows: knit 2 together, slip 1 from the right needle to the left one, knit the next 2 together, slip 1 from the right needle to the left one, knit the next 2 together, slip 1 from the right needle to the left one, knit the next 2 together, slip 1 from the right needle to the left one, knit the next 2 together, slip 1 from the right needle to the left one, knit the next 2 together, slip 1 from the right needle to the left one, knit the next 2 together, slip 1 from the right needle to the left one, knit the next 2 together, slip 1 from the right needle to the left one (**note**: count the last stitch as the 1st of the next 7 stitches)* repeat from * to * until the end of the row before the edge stitch, the last 8 stitches, knit 7 through the front legs, knit 1 through the back leg.

**Row 4 (Back Side):** Knit 7 through the front legs, knit 1 through the back leg, *make 8 new stitches on the right needle as follows: move the working yarn on top of the left needle, then insert the right needle through the backside of this loop from back to front and slip this loop onto the right needle, repeat 7 more times, then knit 1 through the back leg tightly, knit 6 through the front legs, knit 1 through the back leg* repeat from * to * until the end of the row.

**Row 5 (Front Side):** Knit 7 through the front legs, knit 1 through the back leg, *knit 8 through the back legs, then knit the next 1 through the back leg tightly, knit 6 through the front legs, knit 1 through the back leg* repeat from * to * until the end of the row.

**Row 6 (Back Side):** Knit all the stitches through the front legs.

**Row 7 (Front Side):** *Bind off 8 through the back legs, binding off the 1st stitch tightly, as follows: knit 2 together, slip 1 from the right needle to the left one, knit the next 2 together, slip 1 from the right needle to the left one, knit the next 2 together, slip 1 from the right needle to the left one, knit the next 2 together, slip 1 from the right needle to the left one, knit the next 2 together, slip 1 from the right needle to the left one, knit the next 2 together, slip 1 from the right needle to the left one, knit the next 2 together, slip 1 from the right needle to the left one, knit the next 2 together, slip 1 from the right needle to the left one (**note**: count the last stitch as the 1st of the next 7 stitches), knit 7 through the front legs, knit 1 through the back leg* repeat from * to * before the edge stitch, bind off the last 8 as described above in this row.

**Row 8 (Back Side):** *Make 8 new stitches on the right needle as follows: move the working yarn on top of the left needle, then insert the right needle through the backside of this loop from back to front and slip this loop onto the right needle, repeat 7 more times, knit 1 through the back leg tightly, knit 6 through the front legs, knit 1 through the back leg* repeat from * to * until the end of the row before the edge stitch, make 8 new stitches on the right needle as described above in this row.

**Row 9 (Front Side):** *Knit 8 through the back legs, knit 1 through the back leg tightly, knit 6 through the front legs, knit 1 through the back leg* repeat from * to * before the edge stitch, knit the last 8 through the back legs.

**Row 10 (Back Side):** Knit all the stitches through the front legs.

**Repeat rows:** 3-10.

**Bind off after the last row 10 as follows:** Slip the edge stitch onto the right needle, knit the next 1 through the front leg, insert the left needle through the slipped edge stitch, from left to right, and pass it over the knitted stitch, *now there is 1 stitch on the right needle, knit the next 1 through the front leg (now there are 2 stitches on the right needle), insert the left needle through the 1st stitch on the right needle, from left to right, and pass it over the 2nd one* repeat from * to * until the end of the row.

# Pattern 25

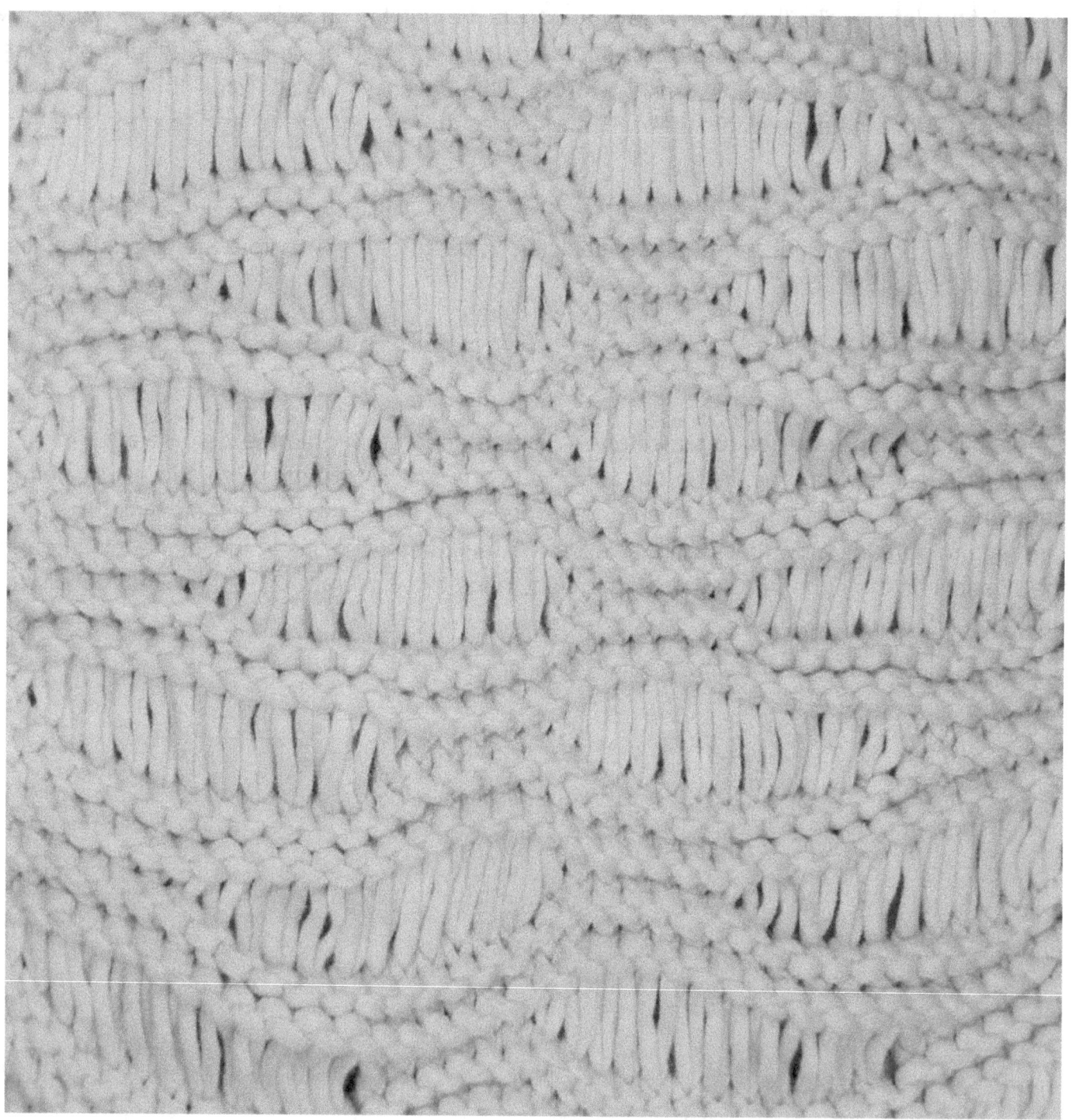

Cast on a multiple of 18, plus 2 edge stitches. Eighteen-stitch repeat. Repeat rows: 2-9. **The edge stitches are not included in the description below and must be added. Slip the first edge stitch; purl the last edge stitch as in knitting through the back leg as follows:** with the working yarn in front of the stitch, insert the right needle through the stitch from back to front, move the working yarn under the right needle and pull it with the needle through the stitch. **Use tape, code, or bulky yarn.**

# Description:

**Row 1 (set up row):** Knit all the stitches through the back legs.

**Row 2:** *Knit 12 through the front legs as follows: yarn over forward (i.e., from yourself), knit 1 through the front leg, then yarn over forward 2 times, knit 1 through the front leg, repeat yarn over 2 times, knit 1 through the front leg 9 more times, then yarn over, knit 1 through the front leg, then knit 6 through the back legs* repeat from * to * until the end of the row.

**Row 3:** *Knit 6 through the back legs, then knit 1 through the front leg, slip 1 yarn over off the left needle and leave it as is, then knit 1 through the front leg, slip double yarn over off the left needle and leave it as is, repeat knit 1 through the front leg, slip double yarn over off the left needle and leave it as is 9 more times, then knit 1 through the front leg, slip 1 yarn over off the left needle and leave it as is* repeat from * to * until the end of the row.

**Row 4:** Knit all the stitches through the back legs.

**Row 5:** Knit all the stitches through the back legs.

**Row 6:** *Knit 6 through the back legs, then yarn over forward, knit 1 through the front leg, then yarn over forward 2 times, knit 1 through the front leg, repeat yarn over forward 2 times, knit 1 through the front leg 9 more times, then yarn over forward, knit 1 through the front leg* repeat from * to * until the end of the row.

**Row 7:** *Knit 1 through the front leg, slip 1 yarn over off the left needle and leave it as is, then knit 1 through the front leg, slip double yarn over off the left needle and leave it as is, repeat knit 1 through the front leg, slip double yarn over off the left needle and leave it as is 9 more times, then knit 1 through the front leg, slip 1 yarn over off the left needle and leave it as is, then knit 6 through the back legs* repeat from * to * until the end of the row.

**Row 8:** Knit all the stitches through the back legs.

**Row 9:** Knit all the stitches through the back legs.

**Repeat rows:** 2-9.

**Bind off after the last row 9 as follows:** Slip the edge stitch onto the right needle, knit the next 1, then insert the left needle through the slipped edge stitch, from left to right, and pass it over the knitted stitch, *now there is 1 stitch on the right needle, knit the next 1 (now there are 2 stitches on the right needle), insert the left needle through the 1st stitch on the right needle, from left to right, and pass it over the 2nd one* repeat from * to * until the end of the row.

# Pattern 26

Cast on a multiple of 3, plus 2 edge stitches. Three-stitch repeat. Repeat rows: 1-4. **The edge stitches are not included in the description below and must be added. Slip the first edge stitch; purl the last edge stitch as in knitting through the back leg as follows:** with the working yarn in front of the stitch, insert the right needle through the stitch from back to front, move the working yarn under the right needle and pull it with the needle through the stitch.

**Knit through the front leg, purl as follows:** with the working yarn in front of the stitch, insert the right needle through the stitch from back to front, wrap the working yarn forward (i.e., from yourself) around the tip of the right needle, then pull the working yarn with the right needle through the stitch. The purl stitch that is worked this way sets up the knit stitch to be knitted through the front leg. **Needles: U.S. no. 4 (3.5 mm). Knit tightly.**

## Description:

**Row 1:** *Knit 3 as follows: knit the first 2 together through the front legs, then knit the next 1 together with the left half of the stitch that lies under the 1st stitch on the right needle received after knitting 2 together (i.e., 1 row below) through the back legs, first moving the front leg of the 1st stitch on the left needle to the back as follows: insert the right needle through the 1st stitch on the left needle from front to back and slip it onto the right needle, thus moving the front leg of this stitch to the back, then return it onto the left needle, inserting the left needle through this stitch straight, from left to right, then insert the left needle through the left half of the stitch that lies under the 1st stitch on the right needle (i.e., 1 row below) and knits this left half of the stitch together with the 1st stitch on the left needle through the back legs, then yarn over forward (i.e., from yourself)* repeat from * to * until the end of the row before the edge stitch, knit the last 3 as described above.

**Row 2:** Purl all the stitches.

**Row 3:** Knit 1, *yarn over forward, knit 3 as described in row 1* repeat from * to * until the end of the row before the edge stitch, yarn over forward, knit 1.

**Row 4:** Purl all the stitches.

**Repeat rows: 1-4.**

**Bind off after the last row 4 as follows:** Slip the edge stitch onto the right needle, knit the next 1, then insert the left needle through the slipped edge stitch, from left to right, and pass it over the knitted stitch, *now there is 1 stitch on the right needle, knit the next 1 (now there are 2 stitches on the right needle), insert the left needle through the 1st stitch on the right needle, from left to right, and pass it over the 2nd one* repeat from * to * until the end of the row.

# Pattern 27

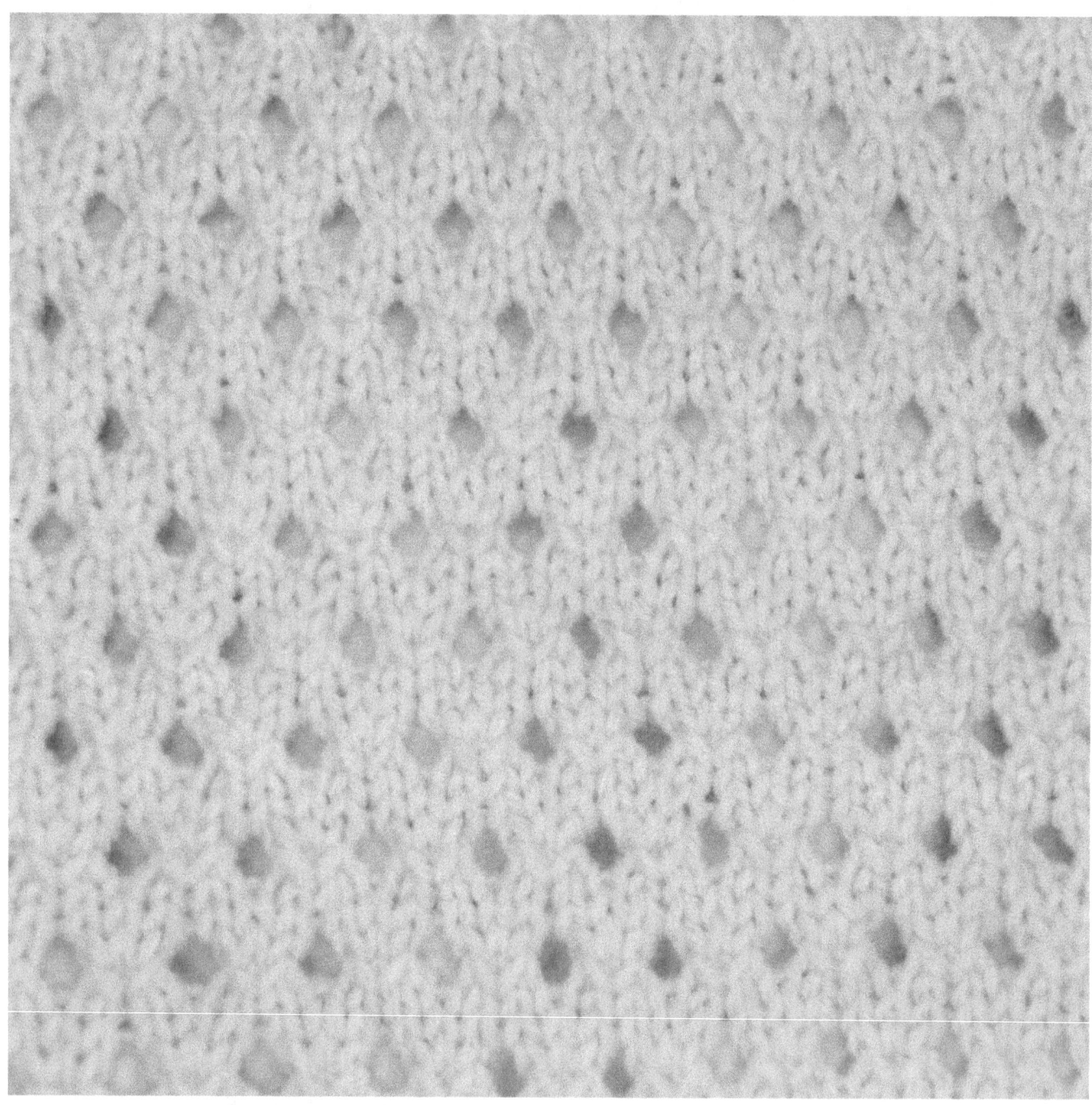

Cast on a multiple of 3, plus 2 edge stitches. Three-stitch repeat. Repeat rows: 1-8. **The edge stitches are not included in the description below and must be added. Slip the first edge stitch; purl the last edge stitch as in knitting through the back leg as follows:** with the working yarn in front of the stitch, insert the right needle through the stitch from back to front, move the working yarn under the right needle and pull it with the needle through the stitch.

**Knit through the front leg, purl as follows:** with the working yarn in front of the stitch, insert the right needle through the stitch from back to front, wrap the working yarn forward (i.e., from yourself) around the tip of the right needle, then pull the working yarn with the right needle through the stitch. The purl stitch that is worked this way sets up the knit stitch to be knitted through the front leg. **Needles: U.S. no. 4 (3.5 mm). Knit tightly.**

# Description:

**Row 1:** *Knit 3 as follows: knit the first 2 together through the front legs, then knit the next 1 together with the left half of the stitch that lies under the 1st stitch on the right needle received after knitting 2 together (i.e., 1 row below), first moving the front leg of the 1st stitch on the left needle to the back as follows: insert the right needle through the 1st stitch on the left needle from front to back and slip it onto the right needle, thus moving the front leg of this stitch to the back, then return it onto the left needle, inserting the left needle through this stitch straight, from left to right, then insert the left needle through the left half of the stitch that lies under the 1st stitch on the right needle (i.e., 1 row below), and knit this left half of the stitch together with the 1st stitch on the left needle through the back legs, then yarn over forward (i.e., from yourself)* repeat from * to * until the end of the row before the edge stitch, knit the last 3 as described above.

**Row 2:** Purl all the stitches.

**Row 3:** Knit all the stitches.

**Row 4:** Purl all the stitches.

**Row 5:** Knit 1, *yarn over forward, knit 3 as described in row 1* repeat from * to * until the end of the row before the edge stitch, yarn over forward, knit 1.

**Row 6:** Purl all the stitches.

**Row 7:** Knit all the stitches.

**Row 8:** Purl all the stitches.

**Repeat rows:** 1-8.

**Bind off after the last row 6 as follows:** Slip the edge stitch onto the right needle, knit the next 1, then insert the left needle through the slipped edge stitch, from left to right, and pass it over the knitted stitch, *now there is 1 stitch on the right needle, knit the next 1 (now there are 2 stitches on the right needle), insert the left needle through the 1st stitch on the right needle, from left to right, and pass it over the 2nd one* repeat from * to * until the end of the row.

# Pattern 28

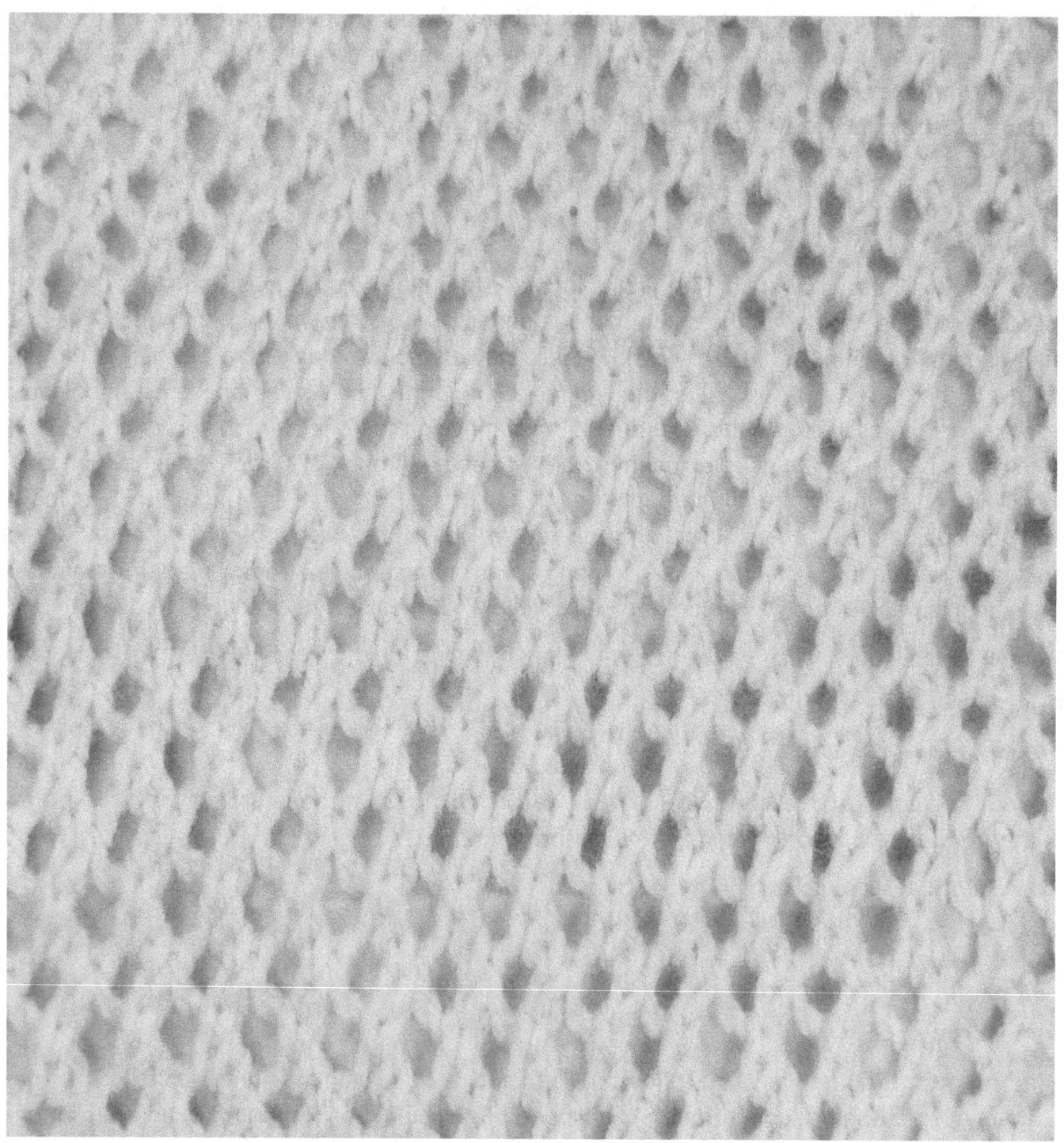

Cast on a multiple of 2, plus 2 edge stitches. Two-stitch repeat. Repeat rows: 1-4. **The edge stitches are not included in the description below and must be added. Slip the first stitch,**

**purl the last edge stitch as in knitting through the back leg as follows:** with the working yarn in front of the stitch, insert the right needle through the stitch from back to front, move the working yarn under the right needle and pull it with the needle through the stitch.

**Knit through the front leg, purl as follows:** with the working yarn in front of the stitch, insert the right needle through the stitch from back to front, wrap the working yarn forward (i.e., from yourself) around the tip of the right needle, then pull the working yarn with the right needle through the stitch. The purl stitch that is worked this way sets up the knit stitch to be knitted through the front leg. **Needles: U.S. no. 4 (3.5 mm). Knit tightly.**

# Description:

**Row 1:** *Yarn over forward (i.e., from yourself), knit 2 together* repeat from * to * until the end of the row.

**Row 2:** Purl all the stitches.

**Row 3:** *Knit 2 together, yarn over forward* repeat from * to * until the end of the row.

**Row 4:** Purl all the stitches.

**Repeat rows:** 1-4.

**Bind off after the last row 4 as follows:** Slip the edge stitch onto the right needle, knit the next 1, then insert the left needle through the slipped edge stitch, from left to right, and pass it over the knitted stitch, *now there is 1 stitch on the right needle, knit the next 1 (now there are 2 stitches on the right needle), insert the left needle through the 1st stitch on the right needle, from left to right, and pass it over the 2nd one* repeat from * to * until the end of the row.

# Pattern 29

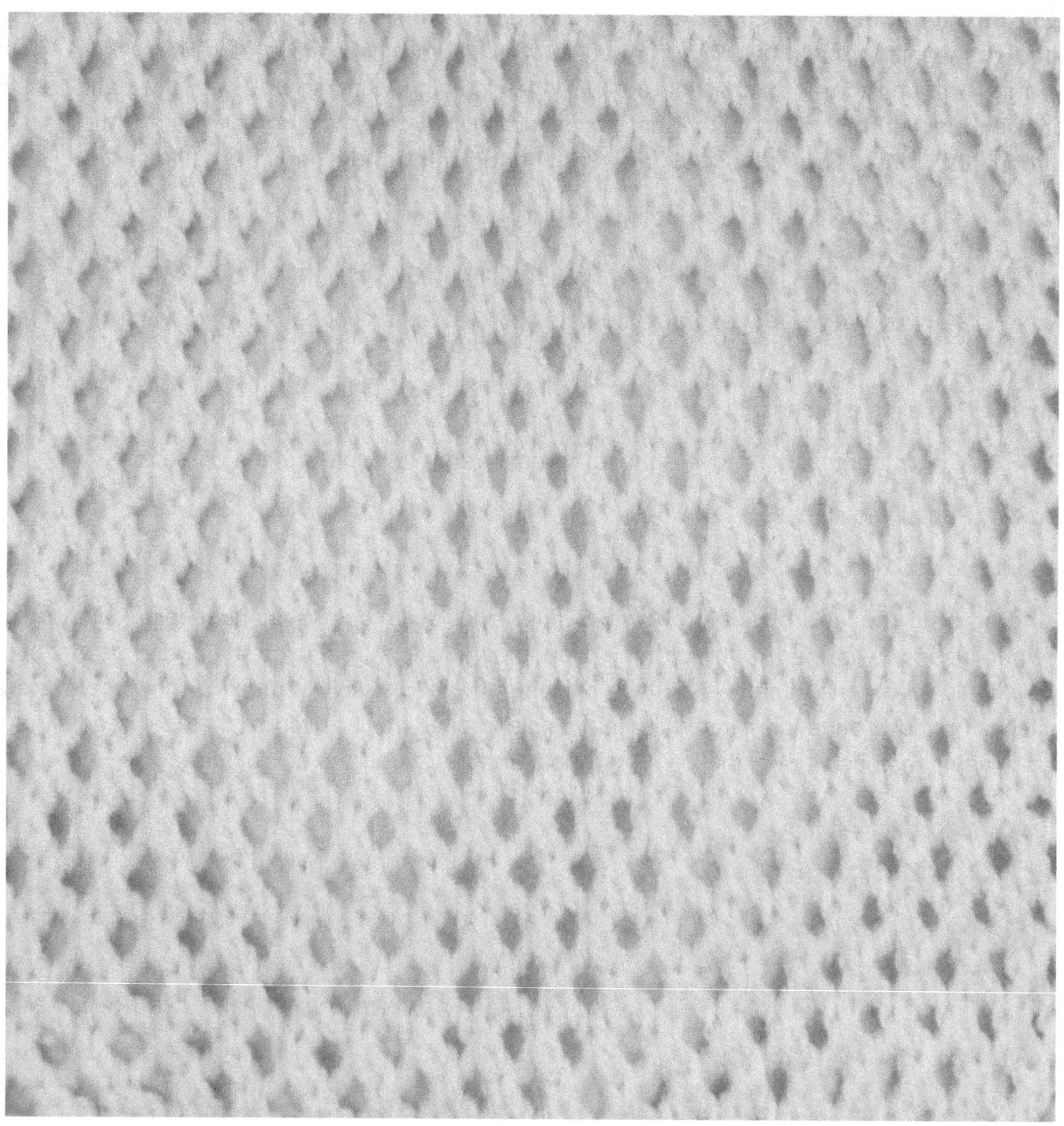

Cast on a multiple of 2, plus 2 edge stitches. Two-stitch repeat. Repeat rows: 1-4.

**The edge stitches are not included in the description below and must be added. Slip the first edge stitch, purl the last one.**

**Knit through the back leg, purl as follows:** with the working yarn in front of the stitch, insert the right needle through the stitch from back to front, move the working yarn under the right needle and pull it with the needle through the stitch. The purl stitch that is worked this way sets up the knit stitch to be knitted through the back leg.

# Description:

**Row 1:** *Yarn over forward (i.e., from yourself), knit 2 together through the back legs* repeat from * to * until the end of the row.

**Row 2:** Purl all the stitches.

**Row 3:** *Knit 2 together through the back legs, yarn over forward* repeat from * to * until the end of the row.

**Row 4:** Purl all the stitches

**Repeat rows:** 1-4.

**Bind off after the last row 4 as follows:** Slip the edge stitch onto the right needle, knit the next 1, then insert the left needle through the slipped edge stitch, from left to right, and pass it over the knitted stitch, *now there is 1 stitch on the right needle, knit the next 1 (now there are 2 stitches on the right needle), insert the left needle through the 1st stitch on the right needle, from left to right, and pass it over the 2nd one* repeat from * to * until the end of the row.

# Pattern 30

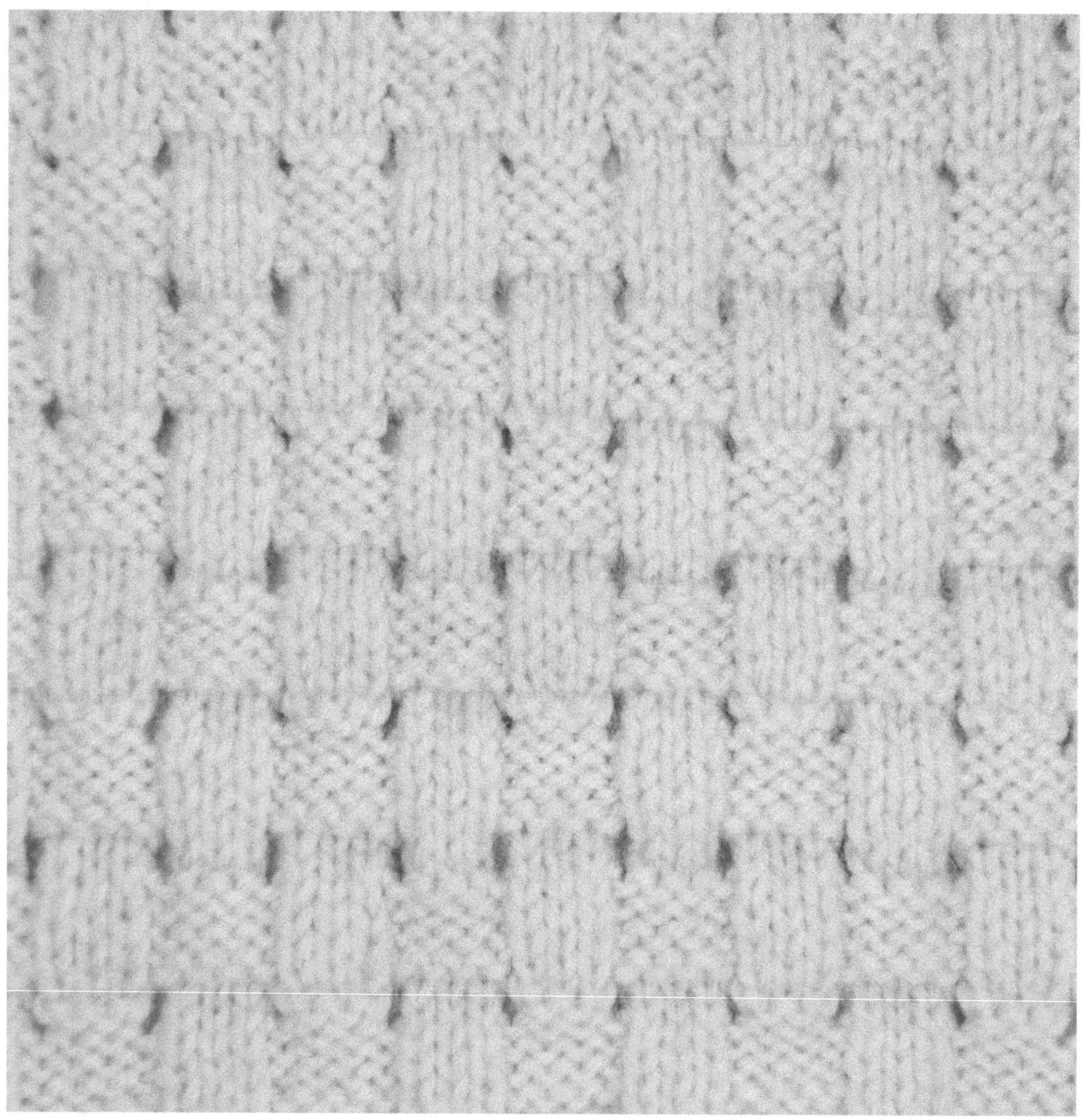

Cast on a multiple of 8, plus 3, and 2 edge stitches. Eight-stitch repeat. Repeat rows: 1-12. **The edge stitches are not included in the description below and must be added. Slip the first edge stitch; purl the last edge stitch as in knitting through the back leg as follows:** with

86

the working yarn in front of the stitch, insert the right needle through the stitch from back to front, move the working yarn under the right needle and pull it with the needle through the stitch.

**Knit through the front leg, purl as follows:** with the working yarn in front of the stitch, insert the right needle through the stitch from back to front, wrap the working yarn forward (i.e., from yourself) around the tip of the right needle, then pull the working yarn with the right needle through the stitch. The purl stitch that is worked this way sets up the knit stitch to be knitted through the front leg. **Needles: U.S. no. 4 (3.5 mm). Knit tightly.**

# Description:

**Row 1:** *Knit 3, purl 5* repeat from * to * until the end of the row before the edge stitch, knit 3.

**Row 2:** *Purl 3, knit 5* repeat from * to * until the end of the row before the edge stitch, purl 3.

**Row 3:** *Knit 3, purl 5* repeat from * to * until the end of the row before the edge stitch, knit 3.

**Row 4:** *Purl 3, knit 5* repeat from * to * until the end of the row before the edge stitch, purl 3.

**Row 5:** Knit 1, *knit 1, knit 2 together through the back legs as follows: insert the right needle through the 1st stitch from front to back and slip it onto the right needle, thus moving the front leg to the back, then return this stitch onto the left needle, inserting the left needle through this stitch straight, from left to right, now knit 2 together through the back legs, yarn over forward (i.e., from yourself), purl 3, yarn over forward, knit 2 together through the front legs* repeat from * to * until the end of the row before the edge stitch, knit 2.

**Row 6:** Purl all the stitches.

**Row 7:** Purl 4, *knit 3, purl 5* repeat from * to * until the end of the row before the edge stitch, the last 7 stitches, knit 3, purl 4.

**Row 8:** Knit 4, purl 3, *knit 5, purl 3* repeat from * to * until the end of the row before the edge stitch, knit 4.

**Row 9:** Purl 4, *knit 3, purl 5* repeat from * to * until the end of the row before the edge stitch, knit 3, purl 4.

**Row 10:** Knit 4, purl 3, *knit 5, purl 3* repeat from * to * until the end of the row before the edge stitch, knit 4.

**Row 11:** Knit 3, *yarn over forward, knit 2 together through the front legs, knit 1, knit 2 together through the back legs as follows: insert the right needle through the 1st stitch from front to back and slip it onto the right needle, thus moving the front leg to the back, then return this stitch onto the left needle, inserting the left needle through this stitch straight, from left to right, now knit 2 together through the back legs, then yarn over forward, knit 3* repeat from * to * until the end of the row.

**Row 12:** Purl all the stitches.

**Repeat rows:** 1-12.

**Bind off after the last row 12 as follows:** Slip the edge stitch onto the right needle, knit the next 1, then insert the left needle through the slipped edge stitch, from left to right, and pass it over the knitted stitch, *now there is 1 stitch on the right needle, knit the next 1 (now there are 2 stitches on the right needle), insert the left needle through the 1st stitch on the right needle, from left to right, and pass it over the 2nd one* repeat from * to * until the end of the row.

# Pattern 31

## Option 1

Cast on a multiple of 4, plus 2 edge stitches. Four-stitch repeat. Repeat rows: 1-4. **The edge stitches are not included in the description below and must be added. Slip the first edge stitch; purl the last edge stitch as in knitting through the back leg as follows:** with the working yarn in front of the stitch, insert the right needle through the stitch from back to front, move the working yarn under the right needle and pull it with the needle through the stitch.

**Knit through the front leg, purl as follows:** with the working yarn in front of the stitch, insert the right needle through the stitch from back to front, wrap the working yarn forward (i.e., from yourself) around the tip of the right needle, then pull the working yarn with the right needle through the stitch. The purl stitch that is worked this way sets up the knit stitch to be knitted through the front leg. **Needles: U.S. no. 4 (3.5 mm). Knit tightly.**

## Description:

**Row 1:** Knit 2 together through the front legs, yarn over forward (i.e., from yourself) 2 times, *knit 2 together through the back legs as follows: move the front leg of the 1st stitch to the back, inserting the right needle through the stitch from front to back and slipping it onto the right needle, then return this stitch onto the left needle, inserting the left needle through the stitch straight, from left to right, now knit 2 together through the back legs, knit the next 2 together through the front legs, yarn over forward 2 times* repeat from * to * until the end of the row before the edge stitch, knit 2 together through the back legs as described above in this row.

**Row 2:** Purl 1, *work double yarn over of the previous row as follows: knit 1 through the front leg, purl 1, then swap the next 2 and purl each stitch as follows: with the working yarn in front of your work, insert the right needle through the 2nd stitch **in front of your work** and slip both stitches off the left needle, then pick up the 1st stitch onto the left needle, inserting the left needle behind the 2nd stitch straight, from left to right, then return the 2nd stitch from the right needle to the left one, inserting the left needle straight, from left to right, now purl each stitch* repeat from * to * until the end of the row before the edge stitch, work the double yarn over of the previous row as follows: knit 1 through the front leg, purl 1, then purl the last 1.

**Row 3:** Yarn over forward, knit 2 together through the back legs as follows: insert the right needle through the 1st stitch from front to back and slip it onto the right needle, then return it onto the left needle and knit 2 together through the back legs, knit the next 2 together through the front legs, *yarn over forward 2 times, knit 2 together through the back legs as described above in this row, knit the next 2 together through the front legs* repeat from * to * until the end of the row before the edge stitch, yarn over forward.

**Row 4:** Purl 1, *swap the next 2 and purl each stitch as follows: with the working yarn in front of your work, insert the right needle through the 2nd stitch **behind your work** and slip both stitches off the left needle, then pick up the 1st stitch onto the left needle, inserting the left needle from left to right, then return the 2nd stitch from the right needle to the left one, inserting the left needle from left to right, now purl each of these 2 stitches, then work the next double yarn over of the previous row as follows: knit 1 through the front leg, purl the next 1* repeat from * to * until the end of the row before the edge stitch, work the last 3 stitches as follows: swap 2 as described above in this row and purl each stitch, then purl the last one.

**Bind off as follows:** After the last row 4, turn your work over. The Front Side: slip all the stitches from the left needle to the right one (as a result, the working yarn is at the end of the right needle), then turn your work over. The Back Side: slip 2 purlwise from the left needle to the right one, insert the left needle through the 1st slipped stitch, from left to right, and pass it over the 2nd one, now there is 1 stitch on the right needle, *slip 1 purlwise from the left needle to the right one, insert the left needle through the 1st stitch on the right needle, from left to right, and pass it over the 2nd one, now there is 1 stitch on the right needle* repeat from * to * until the end of the row.

**Note:** For trimming, bind off using larger needles than the working ones, as this type of binding off creates a tight chain of small stitches.

# Option 2

Knit the same as option 1 using needles U.S. no.10½ (6.5 mm).

# Option 3

Knit the same as option 1 using needles U.S. no. 11 (8 mm).

# Pattern 32

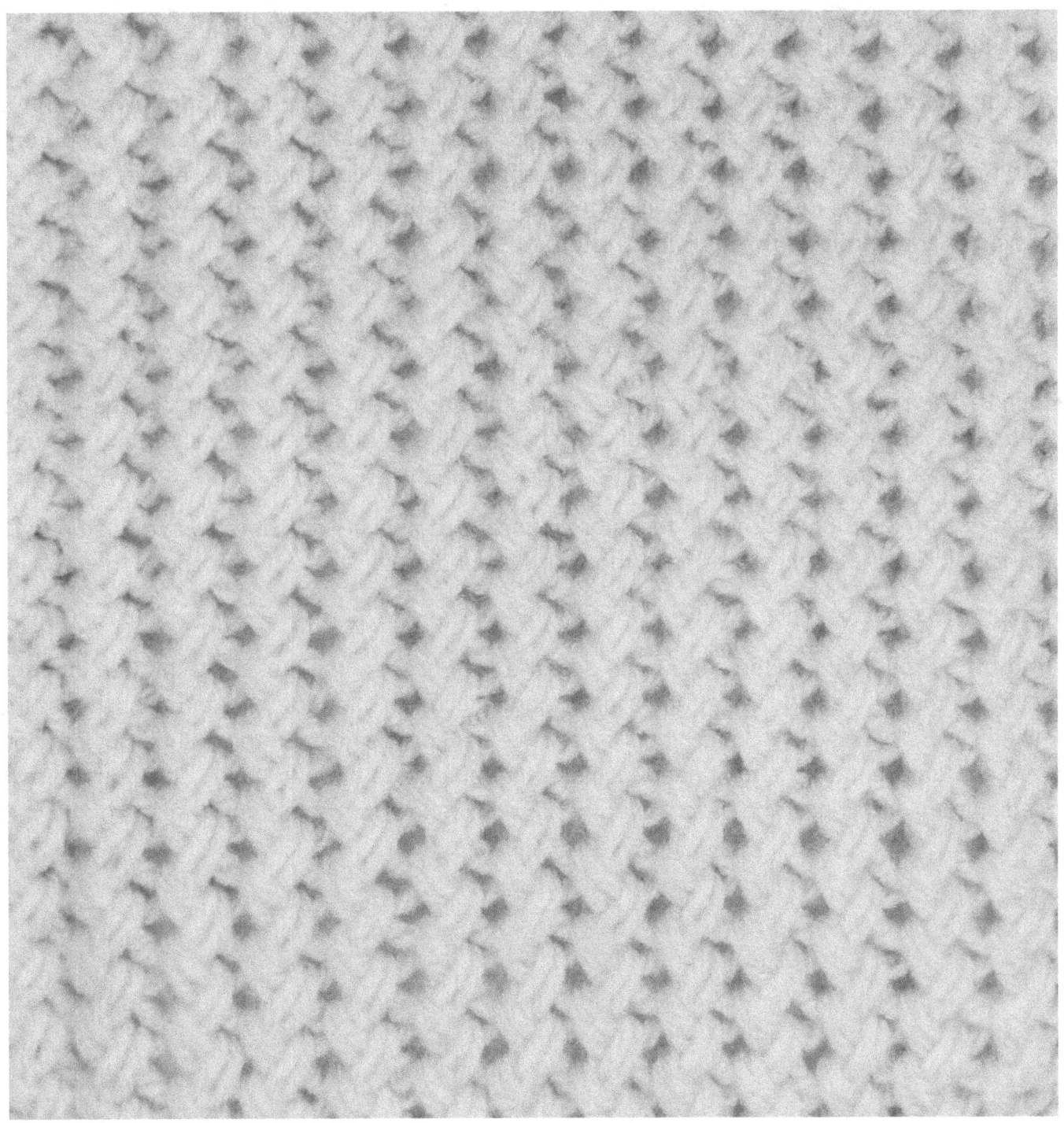

Cast on a multiple of 3, plus 2 edge stitches. Three-stitch repeat. Repeat rows: 1-2.

**The edge stitches are not included in the description below and must be added. Slip the first edge stitch, purl the last one as in knitting through the back leg as follows:** with the working yarn in front of the stitch,

insert the right needle through the stitch from back to front, then move the working yarn under the right needle and pull it with the needle through the stitch.

**Knit through the back legs; purl as in knitting through the front leg as follows:** with the working yarn in front of the stitch, insert the right needle through the stitch from back to front, wrap the working yarn forward (i.e., from yourself) around the tip of the right needle, then pull it with the right needle through the stitch. **The purl stitch that is worked this way sets up the knit stitch to be knitted through the front leg.**

# Description:

**Row 1:** *Yarn over forward (i.e., from yourself), knit 3 together through the back legs—do not release the left needle yet—knit the first 2 stitches together 1 more time * repeat from * to * until the end of the row.

**Row 2:** *Yarn over forward, purl 3 together as described above—do not release the left needle yet—purl the first 2 stitches together 1 more time* repeat from * to * until the end of the row.

**Repeat rows:** 1-2.

**Bind off as follows:** Slip the edge stitch onto the right needle, knit the next 1 through the front leg, insert the left needle through the slipped edge stitch, from left to right, and pass it over the knitted stitch; *now there is 1 stitch on the right needle; knit the next 1 through the front leg (now there are 2 stitches on the right needle), insert the left needle through the 1st stitch on the right needle, from left to right, and pass it over the 2nd one* repeat from * to * until the end of the row.

# Pattern 33

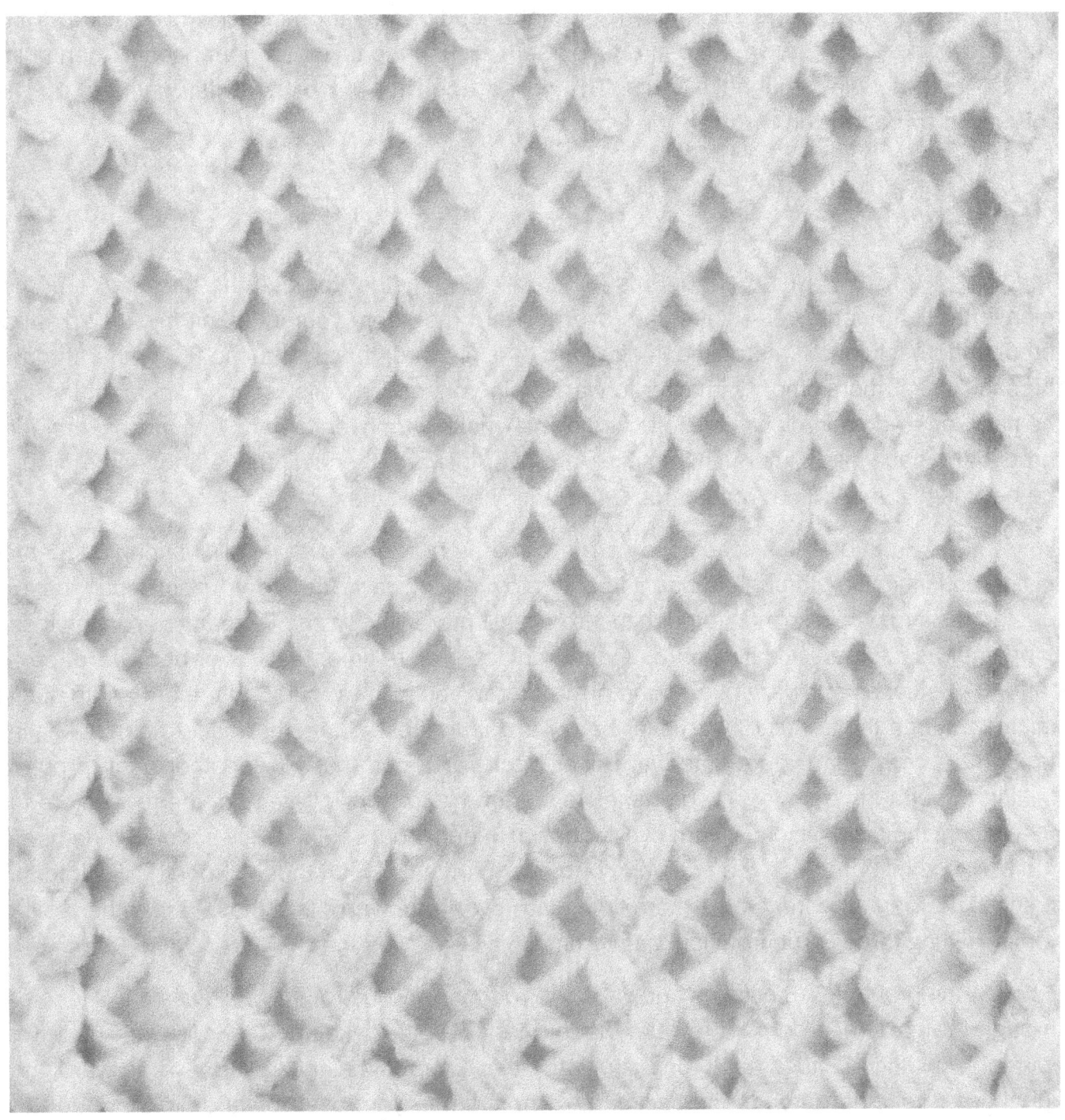

Cast on a multiple of 5, plus 2 edge stitches. Six-stitch repeat. Repeat rows: 2-3. **The edge stitches are not included in the description below and must be added. Slip the first edge stitch, purl the last one as in knitting through the back leg as follows:** with the working yarn in front of the stitch, insert the right needle through the stitch from back to front, then move the working yarn under the right needle and pull it with the needle through the stitch.

**Knit through the back legs; purl as in knitting through the front leg as follows:** with the working yarn in front of the stitch, insert the right needle through the stitch from back to front, wrap the working yarn forward (i.e., from yourself) around the tip of the right needle, then pull it with the right needle through the stitch. **The purl stitch that is worked this way sets up the knit stitch to be knitted through the front leg.**

## Description:

**Row 1 (set up row):** Knit 5 out of 5 as follows: knit 5 together through the back legs—do not release the left needle yet—make yarn over forward (i.e., from yourself), knit these 5 together through the back legs 1 more time, make yarn over forward, then knit these 5 together through the back legs 1 more time, *yarn over forward, knit 5 out of 5 as follows: knit 5 together through the back legs—do not release the left needle yet—make yarn over forward, knit these 5 together through the back legs 1 more time, make yarn over forward, then knit these 5 together through the back legs 1 more time* repeat from * to * until the end of the row.

**Row 2:** Purl 5 out of 6 (5 stitches and yarn over of the previous row) as follows: purl 6 together as if to purl in knitting through the front leg, yarn over **backward (i.e., to yourself)**, purl these 6 together as if to purl in knitting through the front leg 1 more time, yarn over **backward**, purl these 6 together as if to purl in knitting through the front leg 1 more time, *yarn over **backward**, purl 5 out of 6 (5 stitches and yarn over of the previous row) as follows: purl 6 together as if to purl in knitting through the front leg, yarn over **backward**, purl these 6 together as if to purl in knitting through the front leg 1 more time, yarn over **backward**, purl these 6 together as if to purl in knitting through the front leg 1 more time* repeat from * to * until the end of the row before the edge stitch, the last 5 stitches, yarn over **backward**, purl 5 out of 5 as follows: purl 5 together as if to purl in knitting through the front leg, yarn over **backward**, purl these 5 together as if to purl in knitting through the front leg 1 more time, yarn over **backward**, purl these 5 together as if to purl in knitting through the front leg 1 more time.

**Row 3:** Knit 5 out of 6 (5 stitches and yarn over of the previous row) as follows: knit 6 together through the back legs—do not release the left needle yet—make yarn over forward (i.e., from yourself), knit these 6 together through the back legs 1 more time, make yarn over forward, then knit these 6 together through the back legs 1 more time, *yarn over forward, knit 5 out of 6 (5 stitches and yarn over of the previous row) as follows: knit 6 together through the back legs—do not release the left needle yet—make yarn over forward, knit these 6 together through the back legs 1 more time, make yarn over forward, then knit these 6 together through the back legs 1 more time* repeat from * to * until the end of the row before the edge stitch, yarn over forward, knit 5 out of 5 (5 stitches and yarn over of the previous row) as follows: knit 5 together through the back legs—do not release the left needle yet—make yarn over forward, knit these 5 together through the back legs 1 more time, make yarn over forward, then knit these 5 together through the back legs 1 more time.

**Repeat rows:** 2-3.

**Bind off as follows:** After the last row 2, turn your work over. The Front Side: slip all the stitches from the left needle to the right one (as a result, the working yarn is at the end of the right needle); turn your work over. The Back Side: slip 2 stitches purlwise from the left needle to the right one, insert the left needle through the front leg of the 1st slipped stitch, from left to right, and pass it over the 2nd one, now there is 1 stitch on the right needle, *slip 1 stitch purlwise from the left needle to the right one, insert the left needle through the front leg of the 1st stitch on the right needle, from left to right, and pass it over the 2nd one, now there is 1 stitch on the right needle* repeat from * to * until the end of the row.

**Note:** For trimming, bind off using larger needles than the working ones, as this type of binding off creates a tight chain of small stitches.

# Pattern 34

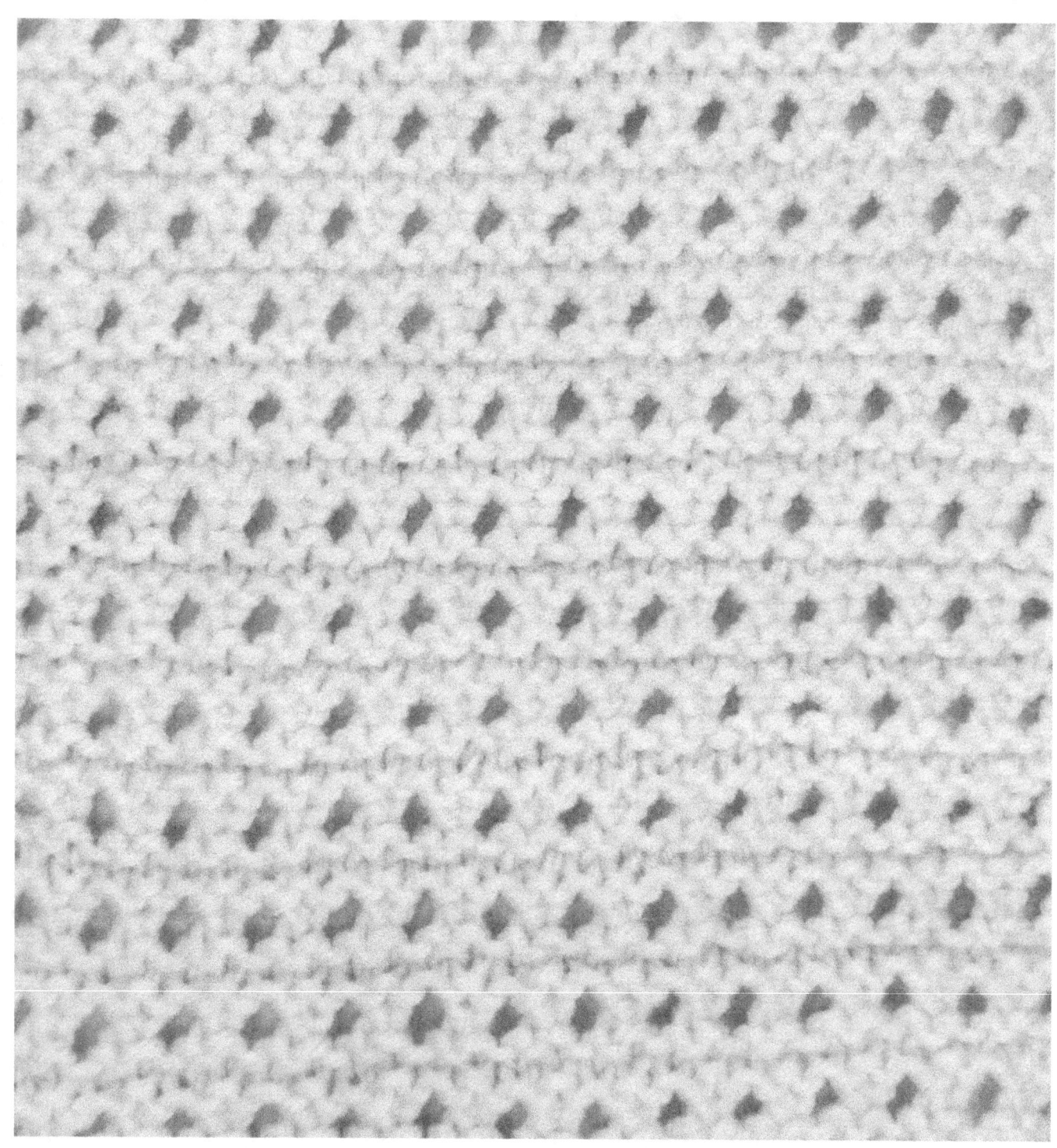

Cast on a multiple of 2, plus 1, and 2 edge stitches. Two-stitch repeat. Repeat rows: 1-4. **The edge stitches are not included in the description below and must be added. Knit the first edge stitch; knit the last edge stitch. Knit tightly.**

**Knit through the front leg; purl as follows:** with the working yarn in front of the stitch, insert the right needle through the stitch from back to front, wrap the working yarn forward (i.e., from yourself) around the tip of the right needle, then pull the working yarn with the right needle through the stitch. The purl stitch that is worked this way sets up the knit stitch to be knitted through the front leg.

## Description:

**Row 1 (Front Side):** Purl all the stitches.

**Row 2 (Back Side):** Purl all the stitches.

**Row 3 (Front Side):** Purl all the stitches.

**Row 4 (Back Side):** Knit 1, *yarn over forward (i.e., from yourself), slip 1 purlwise from the left needle to the right one, knit the next 1, then insert the left needle through the slipped stitch from left to right and pass it over the knitted stitch* repeat from * to * until the end of the row.

**Repeat rows:** 1-4.

**Bind off after the last row 3 as follows:** Slip the edge stitch onto the right needle, purl the next 1, insert the left needle through the slipped edge stitch, from left to right, and pass it over the knitted stitch; *now there is 1 stitch on the right needle; purl the next 1 (now there are 2 stitches on the right needle), insert the left needle through the 1st stitch on the right needle, from left to right, and pass it over the 2nd one* repeat from * to * until the end of the row.

# Pattern 35

Cast on a multiple of 4, plus 2 edge stitches. Four-stitch repeat. Repeat rows: 1-4. **The edge stitches are not included in the description below and must be added. Slip the first edge**

**stitch; purl the last one as in knitting through the back leg as follows:** with the working yarn in front of the stitch, insert the right needle through the stitch from back to front, move the working yarn under the right needle and pull it with the needle through the stitch.

**Knit through the front leg; purl as follows:** with the working yarn in front of the stitch, insert the right needle through the stitch from back to front, wrap the working yarn forward (i.e., from yourself) around the tip of the right needle, then pull the working yarn with the right needle through the stitch. The purl stitch that is worked this way sets up the knit stitch to be knitted through the front leg. **Needles: U.S. no. 7 (4.5 mm). Use a bulky yarn.**

# Description:

**Row 1:** *Knit 2 together, yarn over forward (i.e., from yourself) 2 times, knit 2 together* repeat from * to * until the end of the row.

**Row 2:** *Knit 2 (1 stitch and yarn over of the previous row), purl 1 (yarn over of the previous row), knit 1* repeat from * to * until the end of the row.

**Row 3:** Knit 2, *knit 2 together, yarn over forward 2 times, knit 2 together* repeat from * to * until the end of the row before the edge stitch, knit 2.

**Row 4:** Knit 2, *knit 2 (1 stitch and yarn over of the previous row), purl 1 (yarn over of the previous row), knit 1* repeat from * to * until the end of the row before the edge stitch, knit 2.

**Repeat rows:** 1-4.

**Bind off as follows:** Slip the edge stitch onto the right needle, knit the next 1, insert the left needle through the slipped edge stitch, from left to the right, and pass it over the knitted stitch, *now there is 1 stitch on the right needle; knit the next 1 (now there are 2 stitches on the right needle), insert the left needle through the 1st stitch on the right needle, from left to right, and pass it over the 2nd one* repeat from * to * until the end of the row.

# Pattern 36

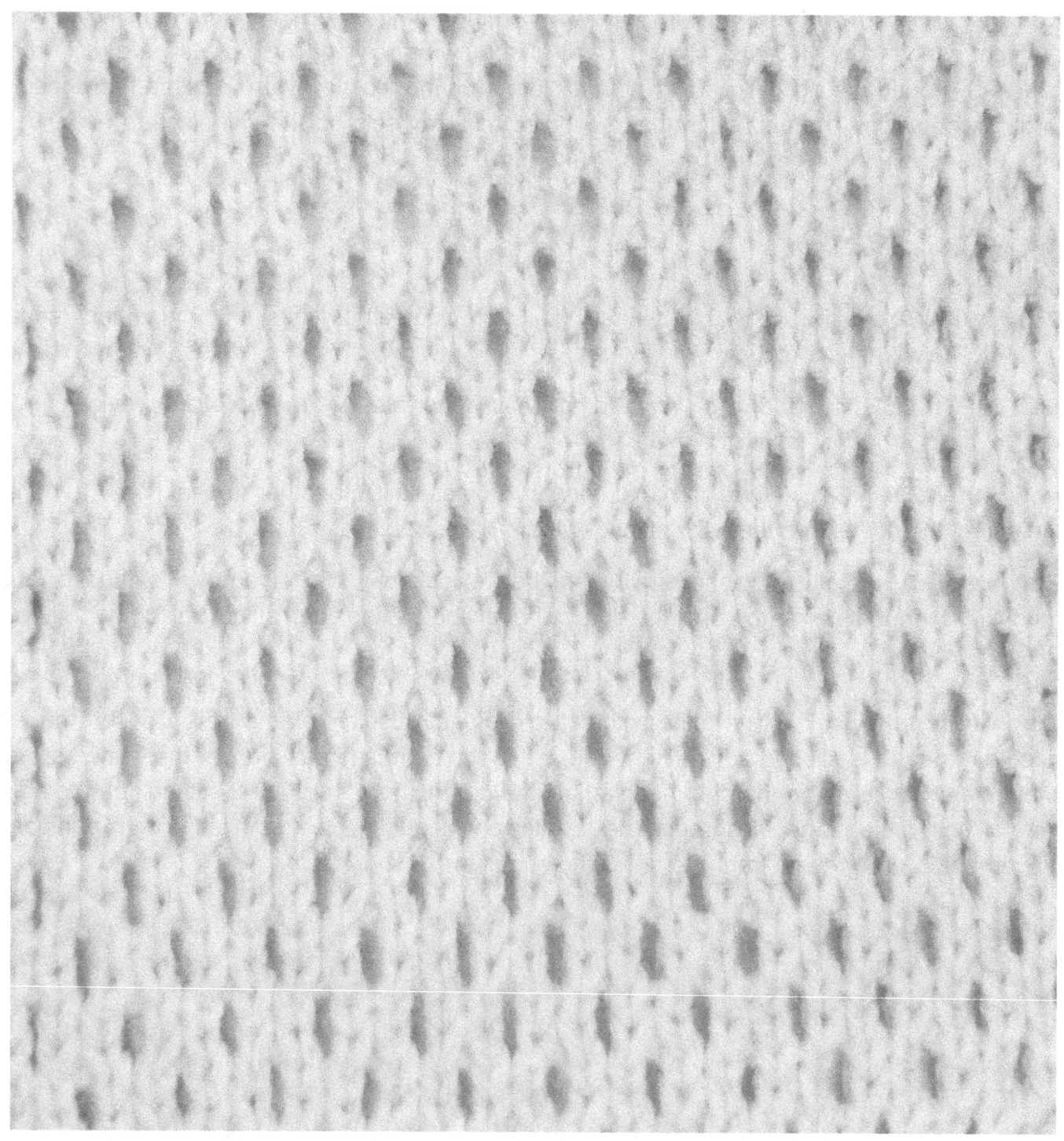

Cast on a multiple of 3, plus 1, and 2 edge stitches. Three-stitch repeat. Repeat rows: 1-4. **The edge stitches are not included in the description below and must be added. Slip the first**

**edge stitch; purl the last one as in knitting through the back leg as follows:** with the working yarn in front of the stitch, insert the right needle

through the stitch from back to front, move the working yarn under the right needle and pull it with the needle through the stitch.

**Knit through the front leg, purl as follows:** with the working yarn in front of the stitch, insert the right needle through the stitch from back to front, wrap the working yarn forward (i.e., from yourself) around the tip of the right needle, then pull the working yarn with the right needle through the stitch. The purl stitch that is worked this way sets up the knit stitch to be knitted through the front leg.

## Description:

**Row 1:** Knit 1, *knit 2 together, yarn over forward (i.e., from yourself), knit 1* repeat from * to * until the end of the row.

**Row 2:** Purl 1, *knit 1, purl 2* repeat from * to * until the end of the row.

**Row 3:** Knit 1, *yarn over forward, knit 1, knit 2 together* repeat from * to * until the end of the row.

**Row 4:** *Purl 2, knit 1* repeat from * to * until the end of the row before the edge stitch, purl 1.

**Repeat rows:** 1-4.

**Bind off as follows:** Slip the edge stitch onto the right needle, knit the next 1, insert the left needle through the slipped edge stitch, from left to the right, and pass it over the knitted stitch, *now there is 1 stitch on the right needle; knit the next 1 (now there are 2 stitches on the right needle), insert the left needle through the 1st stitch on the right needle, from left to right, and pass it over the 2nd one* repeat from * to * until the end of the row.

# Pattern 37

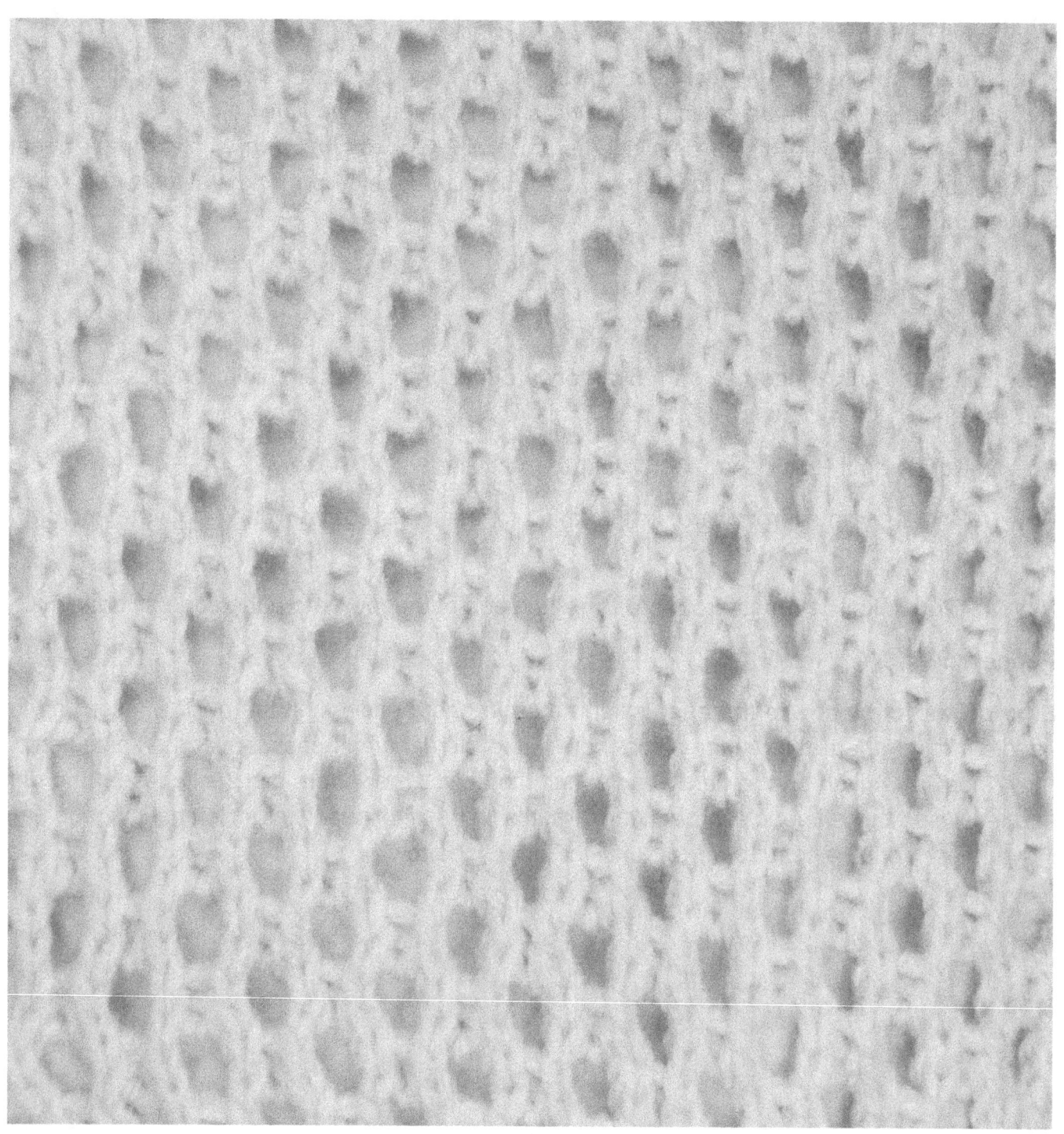

Cast on a multiple of 4, plus 2 edge stitches. Four-stitch repeat. Repeat rows: 3-6. **The edge stitches are not included in the description below and must be added. Slip the first edge stitch, purl the last one.**

**Knit through the back leg, purl as follows:** with the working yarn in front of the stitch, insert the right needle through the stitch from back to front, move the working yarn under the right needle and pull it with the needle through the stitch. The purl stitch that is worked this way sets up the knit stitch to be knitted through the back leg. **Knit tightly.**

# Description:

**Row 1 (set up row):** *Knit 2 together through the front legs, yarn over forward (i.e., from yourself) 2 times, knit 2 together through the back legs* repeat from * to * until the end of the row.

**Row 2 (set up row):** *Purl 1, knit 1 (yarn over of the previous row), purl 1 (yarn over of the previous row), purl 1* repeat from * to * until the end of the row.

**Row 3:** *Yarn over forward, knit 2 together through the back legs, knit the next 2 together through the front legs as follows: slip 1 onto the right needle purlwise, slip the next 1 onto the right needle, inserting the right needle through the back leg from back to front, return both stitches onto the left needle, now knit 2 together through the front legs, then yarn over forward* repeat from * to * until the end of the row.

**Row 4:** Knit 1 (yarn over of the previous row), purl 1, *purl 1, knit 1 (yarn over of the previous row), purl 1 (yarn over of the previous row), purl 1* repeat from * to * until the end of the row before the edge stitch, the last 2 stitches, purl 1, knit 1 (yarn over of the previous row).

**Row 5:** Knit 2 together through the front legs as follows: slip 1 onto the right needle purlwise, slip the next 1 onto the right needle, inserting the right needle through the back leg from back to front, then return both stitches onto the left needle, now knit 2 together through the front legs, yarn over forward, *yarn over forward, knit 2 together through the back legs, knit the next 2 together through the front legs as follows: slip 1 onto the right needle purlwise, slip the next 1 onto the right needle, inserting the right needle through the back leg from back to front, return both stitches onto the left needle, now knit 2 together through the front legs, then yarn over forward* repeat from * to * until the end of the row before the edge stitch, yarn over forward, knit 2 together through the back legs.

**Row 6:** *Purl 1, knit 1 (yarn over of the previous row), purl 1 (yarn over of the previous row), purl 1* repeat from * to * until the end of the row.

**Repeat rows:** 3-6.

**Bind off as follows:** Slip the edge stitch onto the right needle, knit the next 1, insert the left needle through the slipped edge stitch, from left to right, and pass it over the knitted stitch, *now there is 1 stitch on the right needle; knit the next 1 (now there are 2 stitches on the right needle), insert the left needle through the 1st stitch on the right needle, from left to the right, and pass it over the 2nd one* repeat from * to * until the end of the row.

# Pattern 38

Cast on a multiple of 3, plus 2 edge stitches. Three-stitch repeat. Repeat rows: 1-2. **The edge stitches are not included in the description below and must be added. Slip the first edge stitch; purl the last edge stitch as in knitting through the back leg as follows:** insert the right needle through the stitch from back to front, move the working yarn under the right needle and pull it with the needle through the stitch.

**Knit through the front leg, purl as follows:** with the working yarn in front of your work, insert the right needle from back to front through the stitch and wrap the working yarn counterclockwise around the tip of the right needle, then pull the working yarn with the right needle through the stitch. The purl stitch that is worked this way sets up the knit stitch to be knitted through the front leg. **Needles: U.S. no. 4 (3.5 mm).**

# Description:

**Row 1:** *Yarn over forward (i.e., from yourself), slip 1 purlwise, knit 2, then insert the left needle through the slipped stitch, from left to right, and pass it over the knitted 2* repeat from * to * until the end of the row.

**Row 2:** *Yarn over forward, purl 3 together—do not release the left needle yet—purl the 1st stitch 1 more time* repeat from * to * until the end of the row.

**Repeat rows:** 1-2.

**Bind off as follows:** Slip the edge stitch onto the right needle, knit the next 1 through the front leg, insert the left needle through the slipped edge stitch, from left to right, and pass it over the knitted one; *now there is 1 stitch on the right needle; knit the next 1 through the front leg (now there are 2 stitches on the right needle), insert the left needle through the 1st stitch on the right needle, from left to right, and pass it over the 2nd one* repeat from * to * until the end of the row.

# Pattern 39

Cast on a multiple of 4, plus 2 edge stitches. Four-stitch repeat. Repeat rows: 1-4. **The edge stitches are not included in the description below and must be added. Slip the first edge**

stitch, purl the last one as in knitting through the back leg as follows: with the working yarn in front of the stitch, insert the right needle through the stitch from back to front, move the working yarn under the right needle and pull it with the needle through the stitch.

**Knit through the front leg, purl as follows:** with the working yarn in front of the stitch, insert the right needle through the stitch from back to front, wrap the working yarn forward (i.e., from yourself) around the tip of the right needle, then pull the working yarn with the right needle through the stitch. The purl stitch that is worked this way sets up the knit stitch to be knitted through the front leg. **Needles: U.S. no. 4 (3.5 mm).**

## Description:

**Row 1:** Knit 4, *yarn over forward (i.e., from yourself) 2 times, knit 4* repeat from * to * until the end of the row.

**Row 2:** Knit 2, *knit 2 together, knit 1 (yarn over of the previous row), purl 1 (yarn over of the previous row), knit 2 together* repeat from * to * until the end of the row before the edge stitch, knit 2.

**Row 3:** Knit 2, yarn over forward, *knit 4, yarn over forward 2 times* repeat from * to * until the end of the row before the edge stitch, knit 4, yarn over forward, knit 2.

**Row 4:** Knit 3 (2 stitches and yarn over), *knit 2 together, knit 2 together, knit 1 (yarn over of the previous row), purl 1 (yarn over of the previous row)* repeat from * to * until the end of the row before the edge stitch, the last 7 stitches, knit 2 together, knit 2 together, knit 3 (yarn over and 2 stitches).

**Repeat rows:** 1-4.

**Bind off after the last row 4 as follows:** Slip the edge stitch onto the right needle, knit the next 1, insert the left needle through the slipped edge stitch, from left to right, and pass it over the knitted stitch, *now there is 1 stitch on the right needle, knit the next 1 (now there are 2 stitches on the right needle), insert the left needle through the 1st stitch on the right needle, from left to right, and pass it over the 2nd one* repeat from * to * until the end of the row.

# Pattern 40

## Option 1

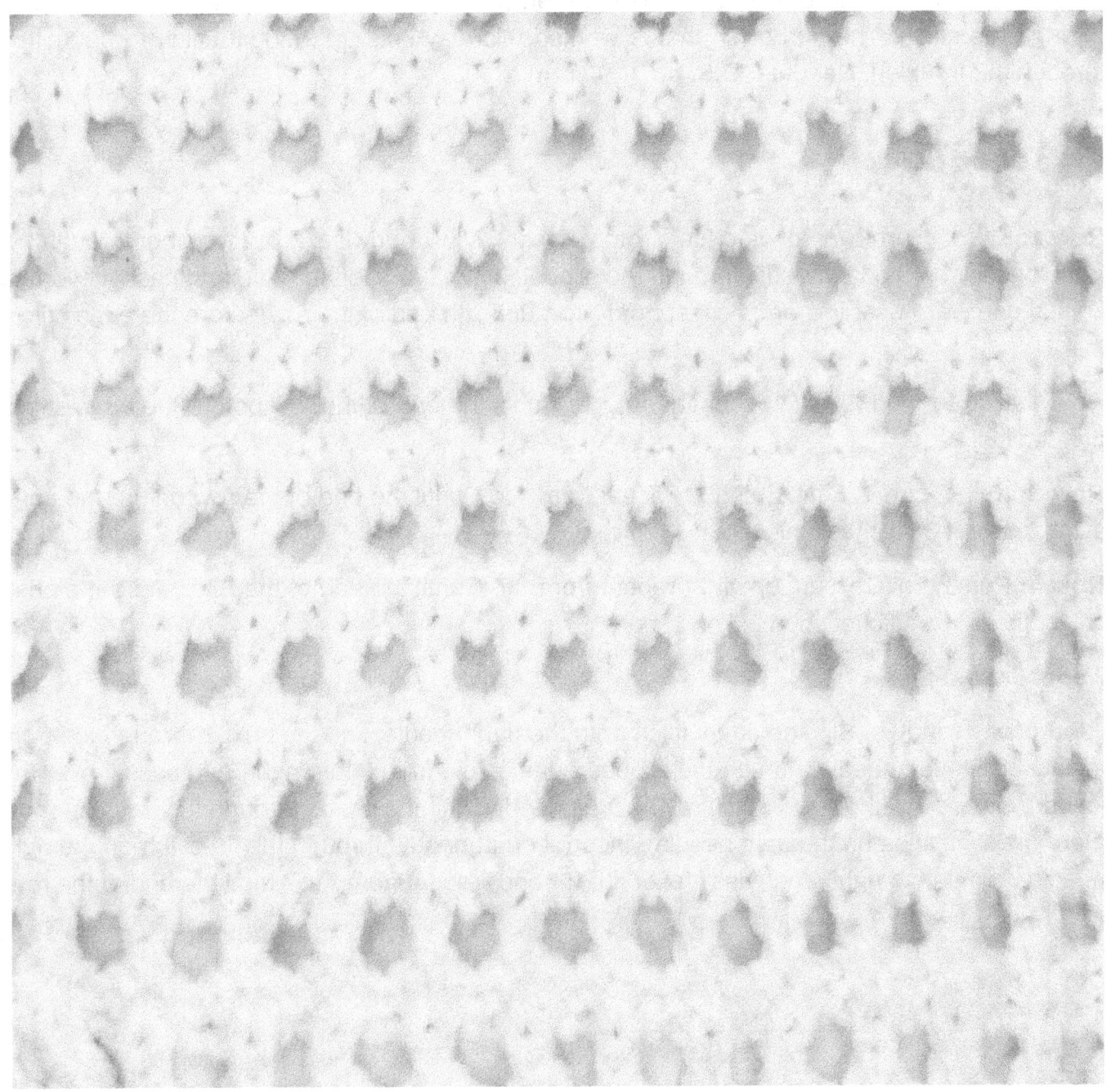

Cast on a multiple of 3, plus 2, plus 2 edge stitches. Three-stitch repeat. Repeat rows: 1-4. **The edge stitches are not included in the description below and must be added. Slip the first**

111

**edge stitch; purl the last edge stitch as in knitting through the back leg as follows:** with the working yarn in front of the stitch, insert the right needle through the stitch from back to front, move the working yarn under the right needle and pull it with the needle through the stitch.

**Knit through the front leg, purl as follows:** with the working yarn in front of the stitch, insert the right needle through the stitch from back to front, wrap the working yarn forward (i.e., from yourself) around the tip of the right needle, then pull the working yarn with the right needle through the stitch. The purl stitch that is worked this way sets up the knit stitch to be knitted through the front leg. **Needles: U.S. no. 6 (4 mm).**

# Description:

**Row 1:** Knit 1, *yarn over forward (i.e., from yourself), slip 1 purlwise, knit 2 together through the front legs, insert the left needle through the slipped stitch, from left to right, and pass it over the knitted one, yarn over forward* repeat from * to * until the end of the row before the edge stitch, knit 1.

**Row 2:** Purl 2, *purl 2, knit 1* repeat from * to * until the end of the row before the edge stitch, purl the last 3.

**Row 3:** Knit 1, purl 1, *knit 1, purl 2* repeat from * to * until the end of the row before the edge stitch, the last 3 stitches, knit 1, purl 1, knit 1.

**Row 4:** Purl 1, knit 1, *purl 1, knit 2* repeat from * to * until the end of the row before the edge stitch, the last 3 stitches, purl 1, knit 1, purl 1.

**Repeat rows:** 1-4.

**Bind off as follows:** Slip the edge stitch onto the right needle, knit the next 1 through the front leg, insert the left needle through the slipped edge stitch, from left to right, and pass it over the knitted stitch; *now there is 1 stitch on the right needle; knit the next 1 through the front leg (now there are 2 stitches on the right needle), insert the left needle through the 1st stitch on the right needle, from left to right, and pass it over the 2nd one* repeat from * to * until the end of the row.

# Option 2

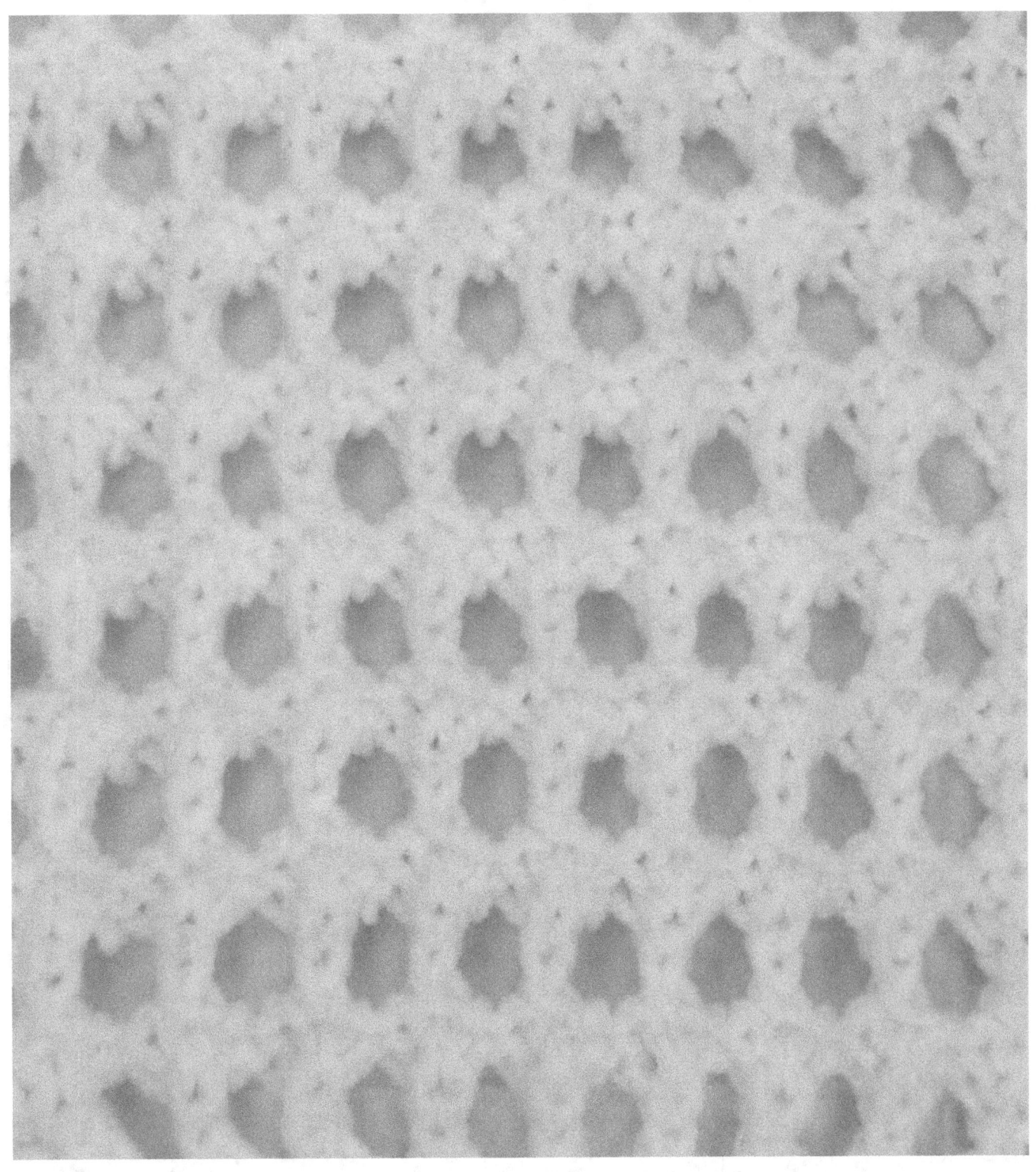

Knit the same as described in option 1 using needles U.S. no. 10 ½ (6.5 mm). **Knit tightly.**

# Option 3

Knit the same as described in option 1 using needles U.S. no. 11 (8 mm). **Knit tightly.**

# Pattern 41

## Option 1

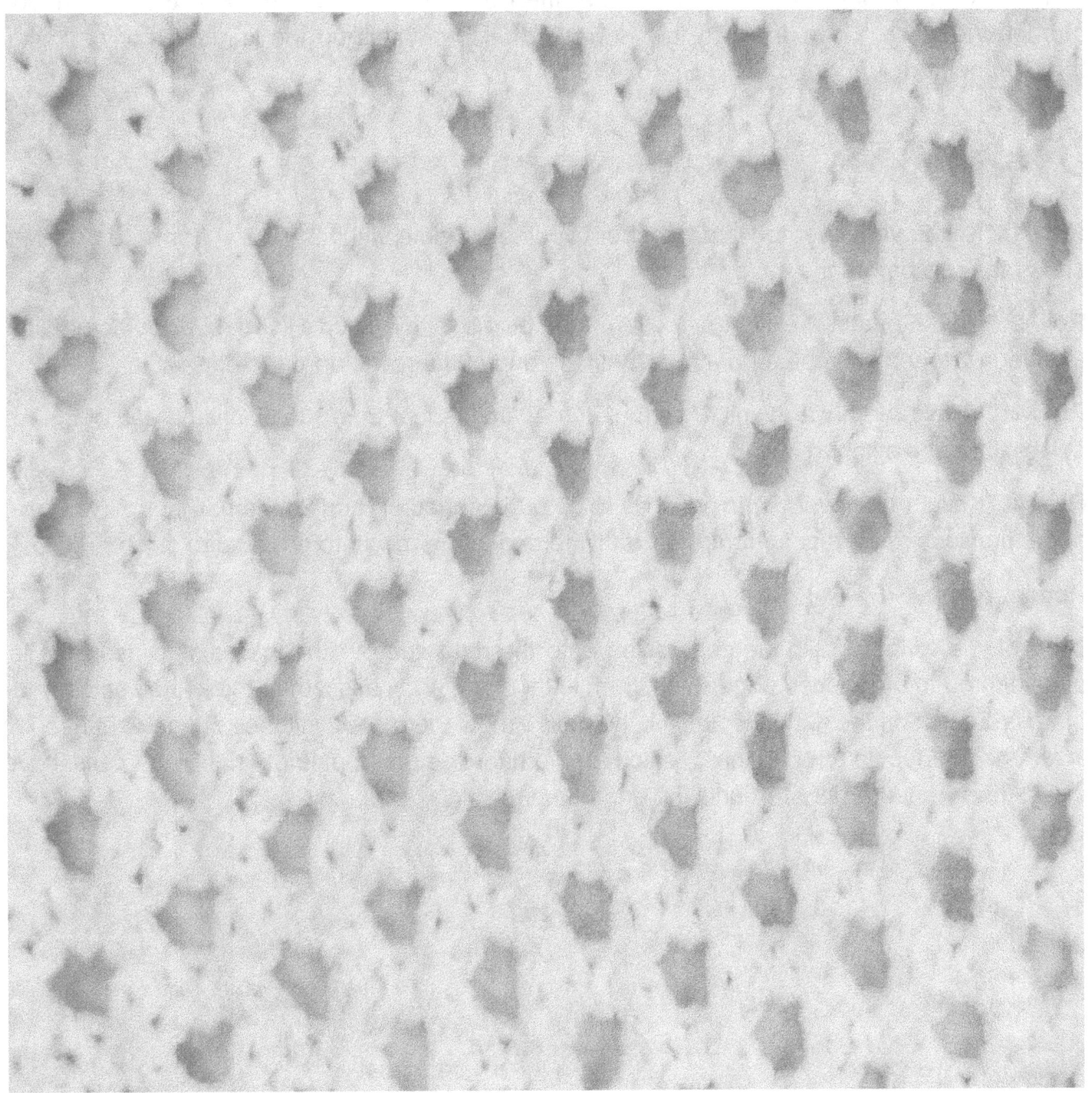

Cast on a multiple of 4, plus 2 edge stitches. Four-stitch repeat. Repeat rows: 1-4. **The edge stitches are not included in the description below and must be added. Slip the first edge**

**stitch, purl the last one as in knitting through the back leg as follows**: with the working yarn in front of the stitch, insert the right needle through the stitch from back to front, move the working yarn under the right needle and pull it with the needle through the stitch.

**Knit through the front leg, purl as follows:** with the working yarn in front of the stitch, insert the right needle through the stitch from back to front, wrap the working yarn forward (i.e., from yourself) around the tip of the right needle, then pull the working yarn with the right needle through the stitch. The purl stitch that is worked this way sets up the knit stitch to be knitted through the front leg. **Needles: U.S. no. 4 (3.5 mm). Knit tightly.**

## Description:

**Row 1:** *Knit 2, yarn over forward (i.e., from yourself) 2 times, knit 2* repeat from * to * until the end of the row before the edge stitch.

**Row 2:** *Purl 2 together, knit 1 (yarn over of the previous row), purl 1 (yarn over of the previous row), purl 2 together* repeat from * to * until the end of the row before the edge stitch.

**Row 3:** *Yarn over forward, knit 4, yarn over forward* repeat from * to * until the end of the row before the edge stitch.

**Row 4:** *Knit 1 (yarn over of the previous row), purl 2 together, purl 2 together, purl 1 (yarn over of the previous row)* repeat from * to * until the end of the row before the edge stitch.

**Repeat rows:** 1-4.

**Bind off as follows:** Slip the edge stitch onto the right needle, knit the next 1, insert the left needle through the slipped edge stitch, from left to right, and pass it over the knitted stitch; *now there is 1 stitch on the right needle; knit the next 1 (now there are 2 stitches on the right needle), insert the left needle through the 1st stitch on the right needle, from left to right, and pass it over the 2nd one* repeat from * to * until the end of the row.

## Option 2

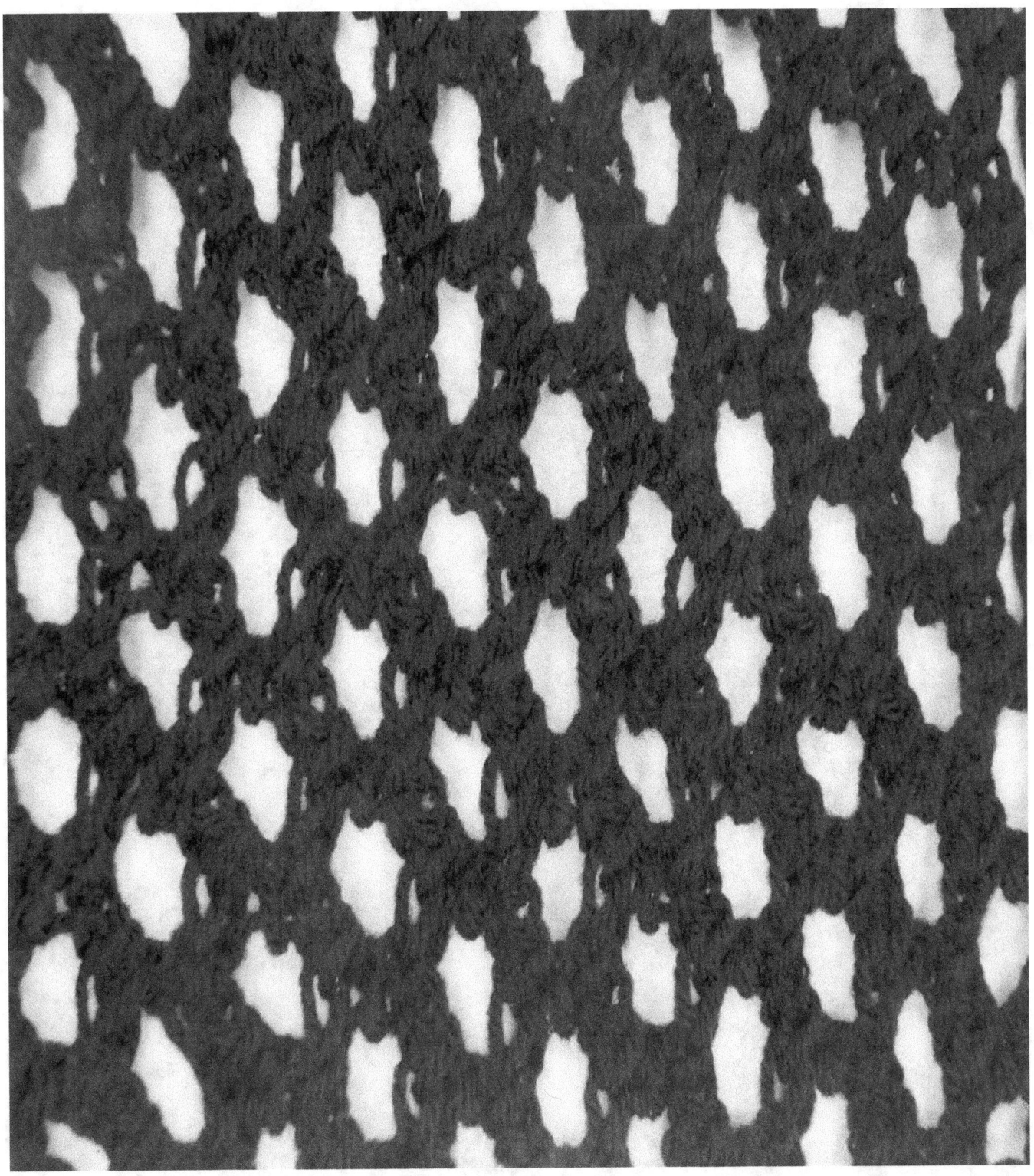

Knit the same as described in option 1 using needles U.S. no. 10 ½ (6.5 mm). **Knit tightly.**

# Option 3

Knit the same as described in option 1 using needles U.S. no. 11 (8 mm). **Knit tightly.**

# Pattern 42

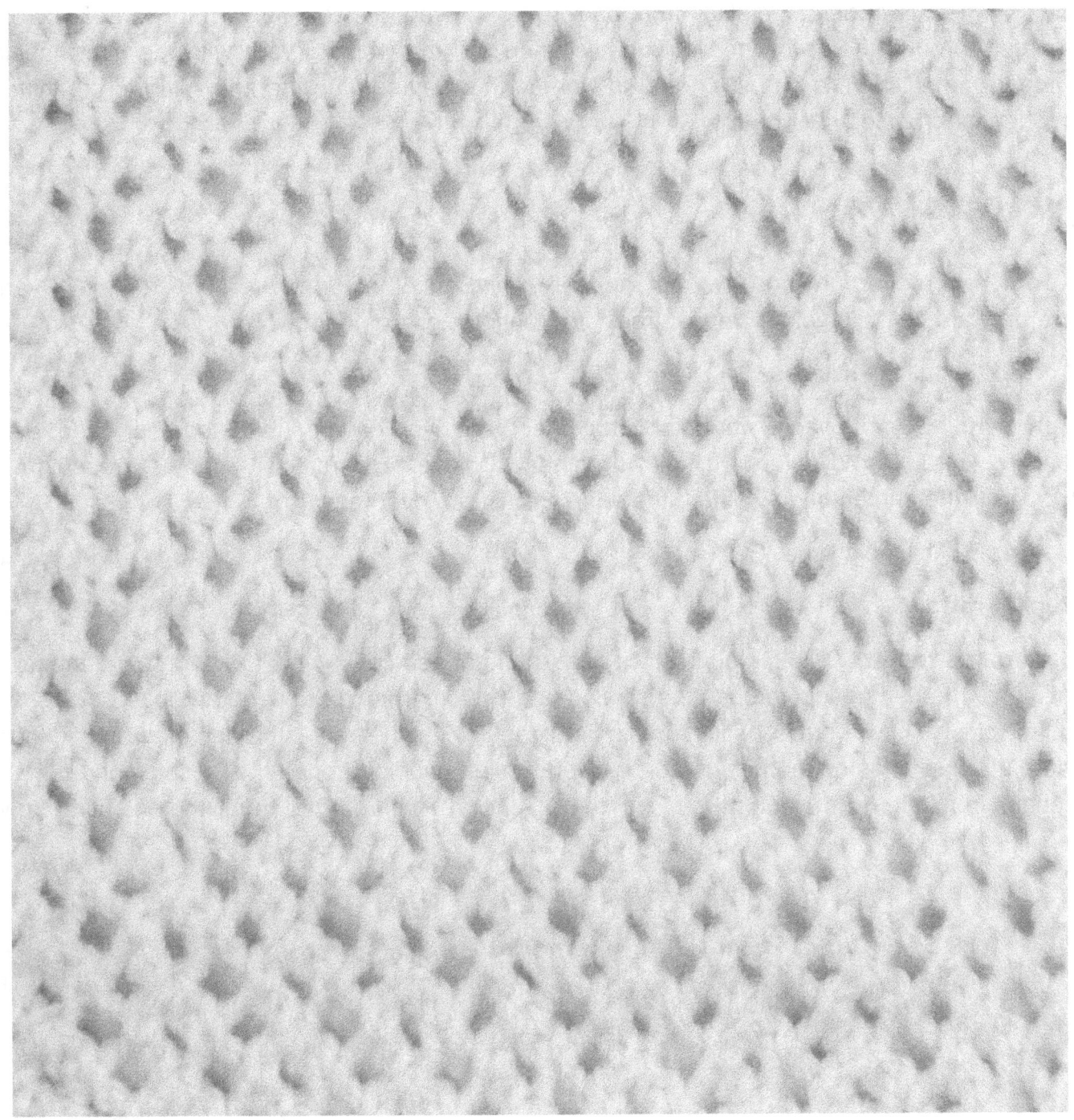

Cast on a multiple of 6, plus 2 edge stitches. Six-stitch repeat. Repeat rows: 1-4. **The edge stitches are not included in the description below and must be added. Slip the first edge stitch, purl the last edge stitch as in knitting through the back leg as follows:** with the working yarn in front of the work, insert the right needle through the stitch from back to front, move the working yarn under the right needle and pull it with the needle through the stitch.

**Knit through the front leg, purl as follows:** with the working yarn in front of the stitch, insert the right needle through the stitch from back to front, wrap the working yarn forward (i.e., from yourself) around the tip of the right needle, then pull the working yarn with the right needle through the stitch. The purl stitch that is worked this way sets up the knit stitch to be knitted through the front leg. **Knit tightly.**

# Description:

**Row 1:** *Yarn over forward (i.e., from yourself), knit 3 together, yarn over forward, knit 1, yarn over forward, knit 2 together* repeat from * to * until the end of the row.

**Row 2:** Purl all the stitches.

**Row 3:** Knit 1, yarn over forward, knit 2 together, yarn over forward, knit 3 together, *yarn over forward, knit 1, yarn over forward, knit 2 together, yarn over forward, knit 3 together* repeat from * to * until the end of the row before the edge stitch, yarn over forward.

**Row 4:** Purl all the stitches.

**Repeat rows:** 1-4.

**Bind off as follows:** Slip the edge stitch onto the right needle, knit the next 1 through the front leg, insert the left needle through the slipped edge stitch, from left to right, and pass it over the knitted stitch; *now there is 1 stitch on the right needle; knit the next 1 through the front leg (now there are 2 stitches on the right needle), insert the left needle through the 1st stitch on the right needle, from left to right, and pass it over the 2nd one* repeat from * to * until the end of the row.

# Pattern 43

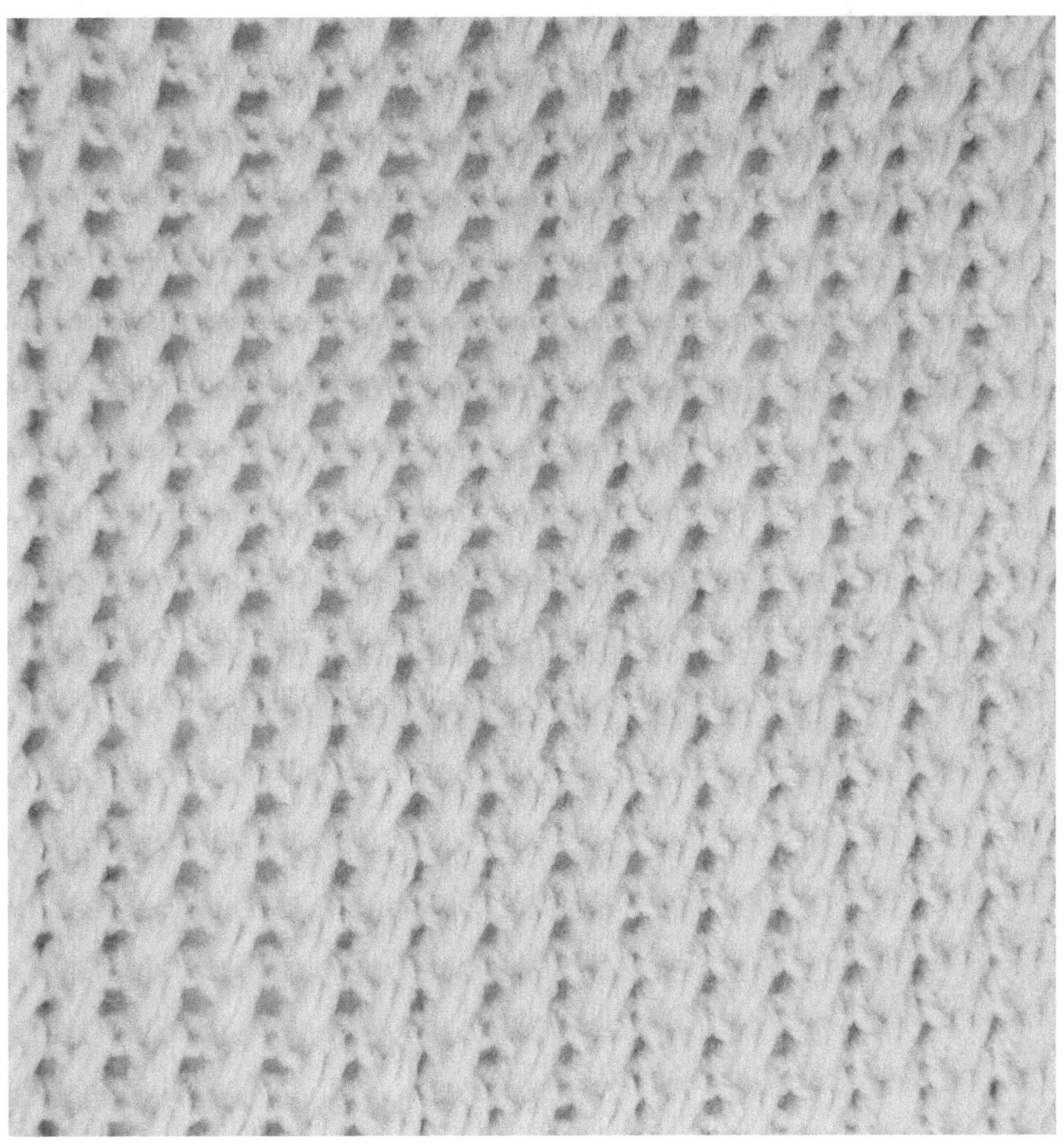

Cast on a multiple 3, plus 2 edge stitches. Three-stitch repeat. Repeat rows: 1-2. **The edge stitches are not included in the description below and must be added. Knit the first edge stitch; knit the last edge stitch.**

**Knit through the back leg, purl as follows:** with the working yarn in front of the stitch, insert the right needle through the stitch from back to front, then move the working yarn under the right needle and pull it with the needle through the stitch. The purl stitch that is worked this way sets up the knit stitch to be knitted through the back leg.

## Description:

**Row 1:** *Knit 3 together as follows: with the working yarn behind your work, insert the right needle from front to back through the space between the $2^{nd}$ and $3^{rd}$ stitches, pull the working yarn through and leave a loop on the right needle, yarn over forward (i.e., from yourself), then knit 3 stitches on the left needle together through the back legs* repeat from * to * until the end of the row.

**Row 2:** Purl all the stitches.

**Repeat rows:** 1-2.

**Bind off after the last row 1 as follows:** Slip the edge stitch onto the right needle, purl the next 1, insert the left needle through the slipped edge stitch, from left to right, and pass it over the purled one, *now there is 1 stitch on the right needle; purl the next 1 (now there are 2 stitches on the right needle), insert the left needle through the $1^{st}$ stitch on the right needle, from left to the right, and pass it over the $2^{nd}$ one* repeat from * to * until the end of the row.

# Pattern 44

Cast on a multiple of 6, plus 2 edge stitches. Six-stitch repeat. Repeat rows: 1-4. **The edge stitches are not included in the description below and must be added. Slip the first edge stitch; purl the last edge stitch as in knitting through the back leg as follows:** with the working yarn in front of the work, insert the right needle through the stitch from back to front, move the working yarn under the right needle and pull it with the needle through the stitch.

**Knit through the front leg, purl as follows:** with the working yarn in front of the stitch, insert the right needle through the stitch from back to front, wrap the working yarn forward (i.e., from yourself) around the tip of the right needle, then pull the working yarn with the right needle through the stitch. The purl stitch that is worked this way sets up the knit stitch to be knitted through the front leg. **Knit tightly.**

## Description:

**Row 1:** *Yarn over forward (i.e., from yourself), knit 3 together, yarn over forward, knit 2 together, yarn over forward, knit 1* repeat from * to * until the end of the row.

**Row 2:** Purl all the stitches.

**Row 3:** Knit 2 together, yarn over forward, knit 1, yarn over forward, knit 3 together, *yarn over forward, knit 2 together, yarn over forward, knit 1, yarn over forward, knit 3 together* repeat from * to * until the end of the row before the edge stitch, yarn over forward.

**Row 4:** Purl all the stitches.

**Repeat rows:** 1-4.

**Bind off as follows:** Slip the edge stitch onto the right needle, knit the next 1, insert the left needle through the slipped edge stitch, from left to right, and pass it over the knitted stitch; *now there is 1 stitch on the right needle; knit the next 1 (now there are 2 stitches on the right needle), insert the left needle through the 1$^{st}$ stitch on the right needle, from left to right, and pass it over the 2$^{nd}$ one* repeat from * to * until the end of the row.

# Pattern 45

Cast on a multiple of 6, **without the edge stitches**. Six-stitch repeat. Repeat rows: 8-9. **Note:** In this pattern, the width knits vertically. Cast on the number of stitches required for the height of your work. Knit the required width vertically, then turn your work horizontally.

**Knit through the back leg, purl as follows:** with the working yarn in front of the stitch, insert the right needle through the stitch from back to front, then move the working yarn under the right needle and pull it with the needle through the stitch. The purl stitch that is worked this way sets up the knit stitch to be knitted through the back leg. **Knit tightly.**

# Description:

**Row 1 (set up row):** Knit all the stitches.

**Row 2 (set up row):** Purl all the stitches.

**Row 3 (set up row):** Knit all the stitches.

**Row 4 (set up row):** Purl all the stitches.

**Row 5 (set up row):** Knit all the stitches.

**Row 6 (set up row):** Purl all the stitches.

**Row 7 (set up row):** Work 6 stitches 10 times as follows: **the Front Side (1st time):** Slip 1, knit 5, then turn your work over; **the Back Side (2nd time):** Slip 1, purl 5, then turn your work over; **the Front Side (3rd time):** Slip 1, knit 5, then turn your work over; **the Back Side (4th time):** Slip 1, purl 5, then turn your work over; **the Front Side (5th time):** Slip 1, knit 5, then turn your work over; **the Back Side (6th time):** Slip 1, purl 5, then turn your work over; **the Front Side (7th time):** Slip 1, knit 5, then turn your work over; **the Back Side (8th time):** Slip 1, purl 5, then turn your work over; **the Front Side (9th time):** Slip 1, knit 5, then turn your work over; **the Back Side (10th time):** Slip 1, purl 5, then turn your work over;

*the Front Side: Slip 1, knit 5, yarn over forward, knit the next 6, then turn your work over;

**Work 13 stitches 8 times as follows: the Back Side (1st time):** Slip 1, purl 12 (including the yarn over of the previous row), then turn your work over; **the Front Side (2nd time):** Slip 1, knit 12, then turn your work over; **the Back Side (3rd time):** Slip 1, purl 12, then turn your work over; **the Front Side (4th time):** Slip 1, knit 12, then turn your work over; **the Back Side (5th time):** Slip 1, purl 12, then turn your work over; **the Front Side (6th time):** Slip 1, knit 12, then turn your work over; **the Back Side (7th time):** Slip 1, purl 12, then turn your work over; **the Front Side (8th time):** Slip 1, knit 12, then turn your work over;

**the Back Side:** Slip 1, purl 5, then slip the next 1 (former yarn over) off the left needle and then slip it down until the row in which this yarn over was made, then turn your work over* repeat from * to * until the last 6 stitches on the left needle at the end of the row.

**Work the last 6 stitches 17 times as follows: the Front Side (1st time):** Slip 1, knit 5, then turn your work over; **the Back Side (2nd time):** Slip 1, purl 5, then turn your work over; **the Front Side (3rd time):** Slip 1, knit 5, then turn your work over; **the Back Side (4th time):** Slip 1, purl 5, then turn your work over; **the Front Side (5th time):** Slip 1, knit 5, then turn your work over; **the Back Side (6th time):** Slip 1, purl 5, turn your work over; **the Front Side (7th time):** Slip 1, knit 5, then turn your work over; **the Back Side (8th time):** Slip 1, purl 5, then turn your work over; **the Front Side (9th time):** Slip 1, knit 5, then turn your work over; **the Back Side (10th time):** Slip 1, purl 5, then turn your work over; **the Front Side (11th time):** Slip 1, knit 5, then turn your work over; **the Back Side (12th time):** Slip 1, purl 5, then turn your work over; **the Front Side (13th time):** Slip 1, knit 5, then turn your work over; **the Back Side (14th time):** Slip 1, purl 5, then turn your work over; **the Front Side (15th time):** Slip 1, knit 5, then turn your work over; **the Back Side (16th Time):** Slip 1, purl 5, then turn your work over; **the Front Side (17th time):** Slip 1, knit 5, then turn your work over;

**Row 8 (Back Side):** *Slip 1, purl 5, yarn over forward (i.e., from yourself), purl the next 6, then turn your work over;

**Work 13 stitches 8 times as follows: the Front Side (1st time):** Slip 1, knit 12 (including the yarn over of the previous row), then turn your work over; **the Back Side (2nd time):** Slip 1, purl 12, then turn your work over, **the Front Side (3rd time):** Slip 1, knit 12, then turn your work over; **the Back Side (4th time):** Slip 1, purl 12, then turn your work over; **the Front Side (5th time):** Slip 1, knit 12, then turn your work over; **the Back Side (6th time):** Slip 1, purl 12, then turn your work over; **the Front Side (7th time):** Slip 1, knit 12, then turn your work over; **the Back Side (8th time):** Slip 1, purl 12, then turn your work over;

**The Front Side:** Slip 1, knit 5, slip the next 1 (former yarn over) off the left needle and then slide it down until the row in which this yarn over was made, then turn your work over;

**The Back Side:** Slip 1, purl 5, yarn over forward, purl the next 6, then turn your work over;

**Work 13 stitches 8 times as follows: the Front Side (1st time):** Slip 1, knit 12 (including the yarn over of the previous row), then turn your work over; **the Back Side (2nd time):** Slip 1, purl 12, then turn your work over; **the Front Side (3rd time):** Slip 1, knit 12, then turn your work over; **the Back Side (4th time):** Slip 1, purl 12, then turn your work over; **the Front Side (5th time):** Slip 1, knit 12, then turn your work over; **the Back Side (6th time):** Slip 1, purl 12, then turn your work over; **the Front Side (7th time):** Slip 1, knit 12, then turn your work over; **the Back Side (8th time):** Slip 1, purl 12, then turn your work over;

**The Front Side:** Slip 1, knit 5, slip the next 1 (former yarn over) off the left needle and then slide it down until the row in which this yarn over was made, then turn your work over * repeat from * to * until the last 6 stitches on the left needle at the end of the row.

**Work the last 6 stitches 17 times as follows: the Back Side (1st time):** Slip 1, purl 5, then turn your work over; **the Front Side (2nd time):** Slip 1, knit 5, then turn your work over; **the Back Side (3rd time):** Slip 1, purl 5, then turn your work over; **the Front Side (4th time):** Slip 1, knit 5, then turn your work over; **the Back Side (5th time):** Slip 1, purl 5, then turn your work over; **the Front Side (6th time):** Slip 1, knit 5, then turn your work over; **the Back Side (7th time):** Slip 1, purl 5, then turn your work over; **the Front Side (8th time):** Slip 1, knit 5, then turn your work over; **the Back Side (9th time):** Slip 1, purl 5, then turn your work over; **the Front Side (10th time):** Slip 1, knit 5, then turn your work over; **the Back Side (11th time):** Slip 1, purl 5, then turn your work over; **the Front Side (12th time):** Slip 1, knit 5, then turn your work over; **the Back Side (13th time):** Slip 1, purl 5, then turn your work over; **the Front Side (14th time):** Slip 1, knit 5, then turn your work over; **the Back Side (15th time):** Slip 1, purl 5, then turn your work over; **the Front Side (16th time):** Slip 1, knit 5, then turn your work over; **the Back Side (17th time):** Slip 1, purl 5, then turn your work over.

**Row 9 (Front Side):** *Slip 1, knit 5, yarn over forward (i.e., from yourself), knit the next 6, then turn your work over;

**Work 13 stitches 8 times as follows: the Back Side (1st time):** slip 1, purl 12, including the yarn over of the previous row, then turn your work over; **the Front Side (2nd time):** slip 1, knit 12, then turn your work over; **the Back Side (3rd time):** Slip 1, purl 12, then turn your work over; **the Front Side (4th time):** slip 1, knit 12, then turn your work over; **the Back Side (5th time):** Slip 1, purl 12, then turn your work over; **the Front Side (6th time):** slip 1, knit 12, then turn your work over; **the Back Side (7th time):** slip 1, purl 12, then turn your work over; **the Front Side (8th time):** slip 1, knit 12, then turn your work over;

**The Back Side:** slip 1, purl 5, then slip the next 1 (former yarn over) off the left needle and then slip it down until the row in which this yarn over was made, then turn your work over* repeat from * to * until the last 6 stitches on the left needle at the end of the row.

**Work the last 6 stitches 17 times as follows: the Front Side (1st time):** slip 1, knit 5, then turn your work over; **the Back Side (2nd time):** slip 1, purl 5, then turn your work over; **the Front Side (3rd time):** Slip 1, knit 5, then turn your work over; **the Back Side (4th time):** slip 1, purl 5, then turn your work over; **the Front Side (5th time):** Slip 1, knit 5, then turn your work over; **the Back Side (6th time):** slip 1, purl 5, turn your work over; **the Front Side (7th time):** slip 1, knit 5, then turn your work over; **the Back Side (8th time):** slip 1, purl 5, then turn your work over; **the Front Side (9th time):** slip 1, knit 5, then turn your work over; **the Back Side (10th time):** slip 1, purl 5, then turn your work over; **the Front Side (11th time):** slip 1, knit 5, then turn your work over; **the Back Side (12th time):** slip 1, purl 5, then turn your work over; **the Front Side (13th time):** slip 1, knit 5, then turn your work over; **the Back Side (14th time):** slip 1, purl 5, then turn your work over; **the Front Side (15th time):** slip 1, knit 5, then turn your work over; **the Back Side (16th Time):** slip 1, purl 5, then turn your work over; **the Front Side (17th time):** slip 1, knit 5, then turn your work over;

**Repeat rows:** 8-9.

**Note:** Bind off after the last row 8 and 5 extra rows, for symmetry with the first 6 rows at the beginning of your work.

**the last row 8:** Work the last 6 stitches 10 times, instead of 17 as usual, as follows: **the Back Side (1st time):** slip 1, purl 5, then turn your work over; **the Front Side (2nd time):** slip 1, knit 5, then turn your work over; **the Back Side (3rd time):** slip 1, purl 5, then turn your work over; **the Front Side (4th time):** slip 1, knit 5, then turn your work over; **the Back Side (5th time):** slip 1, purl 5, then turn your work over; **the Front Side (6th time):** slip 1, knit 5, then turn your work over; **the Back Side (7th time):** slip 1, purl 5, then turn your work over; **the Front Side (8th time):** slip 1, knit 5, then turn your work over; **the Back Side (9th time):** slip 1, purl 5, then turn your work over; **the Front Side (10th time): slip 1, knit all the stitches until the end of the row, thus connecting all separate stitches in one row.** work 5 rows for symmetry with the first 6 rows as follows: **Row 1 (Back Side):** Purl all the stitches; **Row 2 (Front Side):** Knit all the stitches; **Row 3 (Back Side):** Purl all the stitches; **Row 4 (Front Side):** Knit all the stitches; **Row 5 (Back Side):** Purl all the stitches.

**Bind off on the Front Side as follows:** Slip 1 onto the right needle, knit the next 1, insert the left needle through the slipped stitch, from left to right, and pass it over the knitted stitch, *now there is 1 stitch on the right needle, knit the next 1 (now there are 2 stitches on the right needle), insert the left needle through the 1st stitch on the right needle, from left to right, and pass it over the 2nd one* repeat from * to * until the end of the row.

# Pattern 46

Cast on a multiple of 3, plus 2 edge stitches. Three-stitch repeat. Repeat rows: 1-2. **The edge stitches are not included in the description below and must be added. Knit the first edge stitch through the front leg; knit the last edge stitch through the front leg.**

**Knit through the front leg, purl as follows:** with the working yarn in front of the stitch, insert the right needle through the stitch from back to front, wrap the working yarn forward (i.e., from yourself) around the tip of the right needle, then pull the working yarn with the right needle through the stitch. The purl stitch that is worked this way sets up the knit stitch to be knitted through the front leg. **Needles: U.S. no. 4 (3.5 mm).**

**Note:** Control tension of the working yarn. Knit tightly.

## Description:

**Row 1:** *Yarn over forward (i.e., from yourself), with the working yarn **behind your work,** slip 1 purlwise, knit the next 2 through the front legs, then insert the left needle through the slipped stitch, from left to right, and pass it over the 2 knitted stitches* repeat from * to * until the end of the row.

**Row 2:** *Yarn over forward, with the working yarn **in front of your work,** slip 1 purlwise, purl the next 2, then insert the left needle through the slipped stitch, from left to right, and pass it over the 2 worked stitches* repeat from * to * until the end of the row.

**Repeat rows:** 1-2.

**Bind off as follows:** Slip the edge stitch onto the right needle, knit the next 1, insert the left needle through the slipped edge stitch, from left to right, and pass it over the knitted stitch; *now there is 1 stitch on the right needle; knit the next 1 (now there are 2 stitches on the right needle), insert the left needle through the 1st stitch on the right needle, from left to right, and pass it over the 2nd one* repeat from * to * until the end of the row.

# Pattern 47

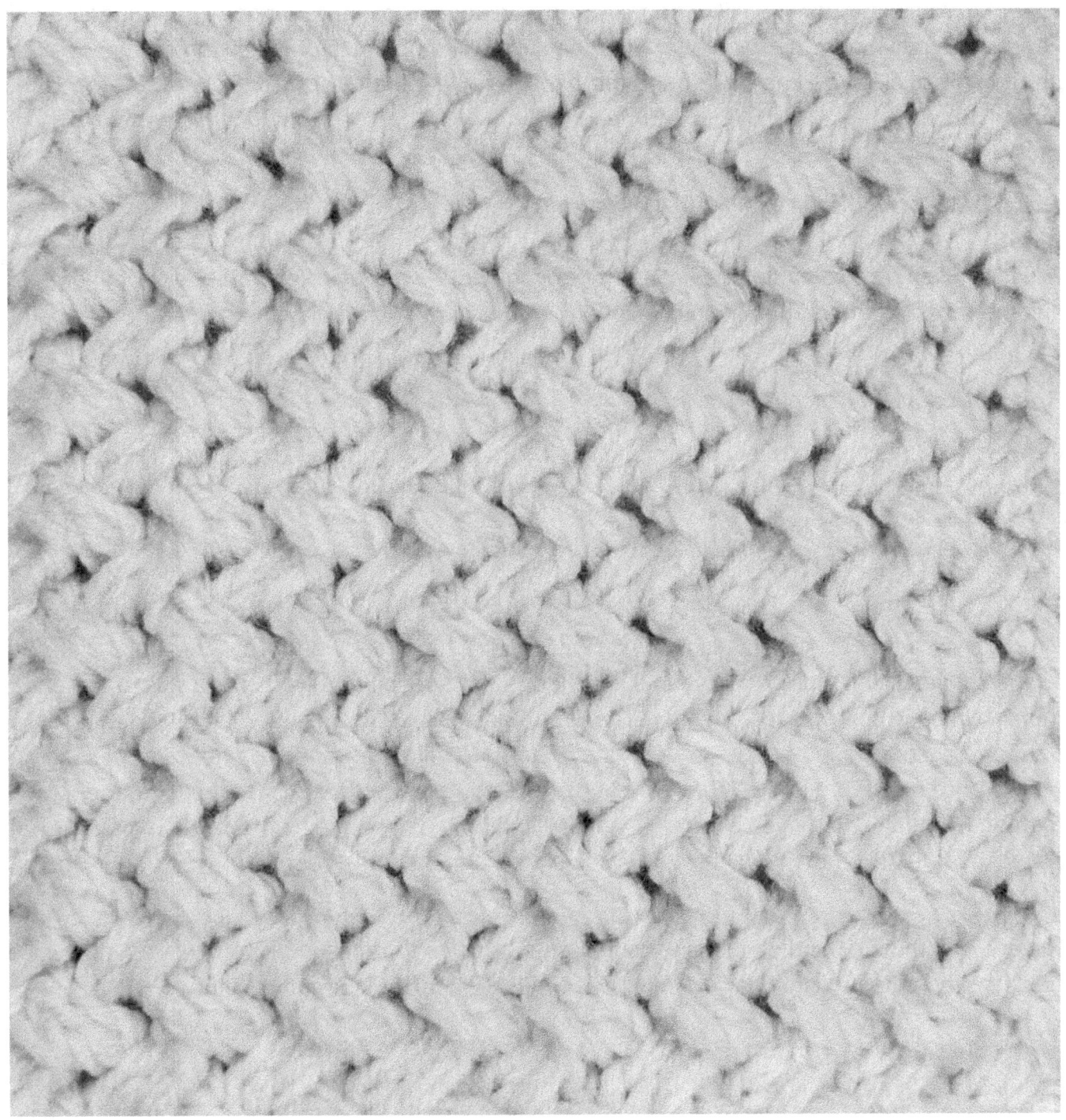

Cast on a multiple of 4, plus 2, and 2 edge stitches. Four-stitch repeat. Repeat rows: 1-4. **The edge stitches are not included in the description below and must be added. Slip the first**

edge stitch, purl the last one as if to purl in knitting through the back leg as described below.

**Knit through the back leg, purl as follows:** with the working yarn in front of the stitch, insert the right needle through the stitch from back to front, then move the working yarn under the right needle and pull it with the needle through the stitch. The purl stitch that is worked this way sets up the knit stitch to be knitted through the back leg. **Needles: U.S. no. 10 ½ (6.5 mm). Use a bulky yarn.**

## Description:

**Row 1:** *Slip 2 onto a cable needle in front of your work, yarn over forward (i.e., from yourself), knit the next 2 together, then knit the slipped 2* repeat from * to * until the end of the row before the edge stitch, knit the last 2.

**Row 2:** Purl all the stitches.

**Row 3:** Knit 2, *slip 2 onto a cable needle behind your work, knit the next 2, then knit the slipped 2 together, then yarn over forward* repeat from * to * until the end of the row.

**Row 4:** Purl all the stitches.

**Repeat rows:** 1-4.

**Bind off as follows:** After the last row 3 (Front Side), turn your work over. The Back Side: Slip all the stitches from the left needle to the right one (as a result, the working yarn is at the end of the right needle); turn your work over. The Front Side: Slip 2 purlwise from the left needle to the right one, insert the left needle through the 1st slipped stitch, from left to right, and pass it over the 2nd one (now there is 1 stitch on the right needle), *slip 1 purlwise from the left needle to the right one, insert the left needle through the 1st stitch on the right needle, from left to the right, and pass it over the 2nd one (now there is 1 stitch on the right needle)* repeat from * to * until the end of the row.

**Note:** For trimming, bind off loosely, using larger needles than the working ones, as this type of binding off creates a tight chain of small edge stitches that look already finished.

# Pattern 48

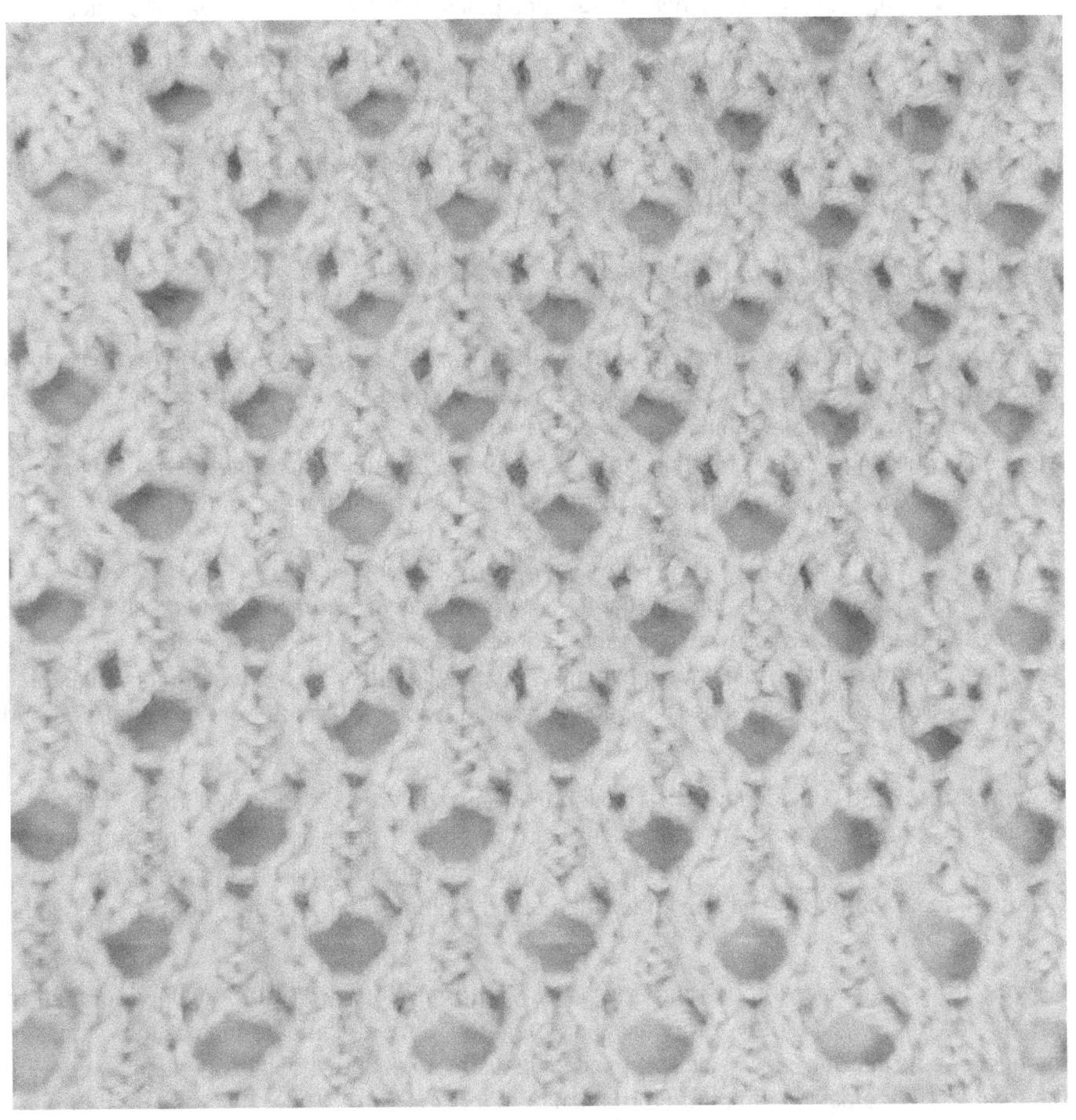

Cast on a multiple of 6, plus 2 edge stitches. Six-stitch repeat. Repeat rows: 1-8.

**The edge stitches are not included in the description below and must be added. Slip the first edge stitch, purl the last one as in knitting through the back leg as follows:** with the working yarn in front of the stitch, insert the right needle through the stitch from back to front, move the working yarn under the right needle and pull it with the needle through the stitch.

**Knit through the front leg, purl as follows:** with the working yarn in front of the stitch, insert the right needle through the stitch from back to front, wrap the working yarn forward (i.e., from yourself) around the tip of the right needle, then pull the working yarn with the right needle through the stitch. The purl stitch that is worked this way sets up the knit stitch to be knitted through the front leg. **Knit tightly.**

## Description:

**Row 1:** *Purl 1 through the front leg, **yarn over forward (i.e., from yourself)**, knit 2 together through the back legs as follow: insert the right needle through the 1st stitch from left to right and slip it onto the right needle, thus moving the front leg to the back, then return this stitch onto the left needle, now knit 2 together through the back legs, knit 2 together through the front legs, **yarn over forward**, purl 1 through the front leg* repeat from * to * until the end of the row.

**Row 2:** *Knit 1, purl 4, knit 1* repeat from * to * until the end of the row.

**Row 3:** *Purl 1, knit 2 together through the front legs, **yarn over forward 2 times**, knit 2 together through the back legs as follows: insert the right needle through the 1st stitch from left to right and slip it onto the right needle, thus moving the front leg to the back, then return this stitch onto the left needle, now knit 2 together through the back legs, purl 1* repeat from * to * until the end of the row.

**Row 4:** *Knit 1, purl 1, work double yarn over of the previous row as follows: purl 1 as in knitting through the back leg (i.e., with the working yarn in front of the stitch, insert the right needle through the stitch from back to front, move the working yarn under the right needle and pull it with the needle through the stitch), knit 1, then purl the next 1, knit 1* repeat from * to * until the end of the row.

**Row 5:** *Knit 2 together through the front legs, **yarn over forward**, purl 2 tightly (each stitch through the front leg), **yarn over forward**, knit 2 together through the back legs as follows: insert the right needle through the 1st stitch from left to right and slip it onto the right needle, thus moving the front leg to the back, then return this stitch onto the left needle, now knit 2 together through the back legs* repeat from * to * until the end of the row.

**Row 6:** *Purl 2, knit 2, purl 2* repeat from * to * until the end of the row.

**Row 7:** *Yarn over forward, knit 2 together through the back legs as follows: insert the right needle through the 1st stitch from left to right and slip it onto the right needle, thus moving the front leg to the back, then return this stitch onto the left needle, now knit 2 together through the back legs, purl 2, knit 2 together through the front legs, yarn over forward* repeat from * to * until the end of the row.

**Row 8:** *Knit 1 (yarn over of the previous row), purl 1, knit 2, purl 1, purl 1 (yarn over of the previous row) as if to purl in knitting through the back leg* repeat from * to * until the end of the row.

**Repeat rows: 1-8.**

**Bind off as follows:** Slip the edge stitch onto the right needle, knit 1, then pass the slipped edge stitch over the knitted one, *now there is 1 stitch on the right needle, knit the next 1, insert the left needle through the 1$^{st}$ stitch on the right needle, from left to the right, and pass it over the 2$^{nd}$ one* repeat from * to * until the end of the row.

# Pattern 49

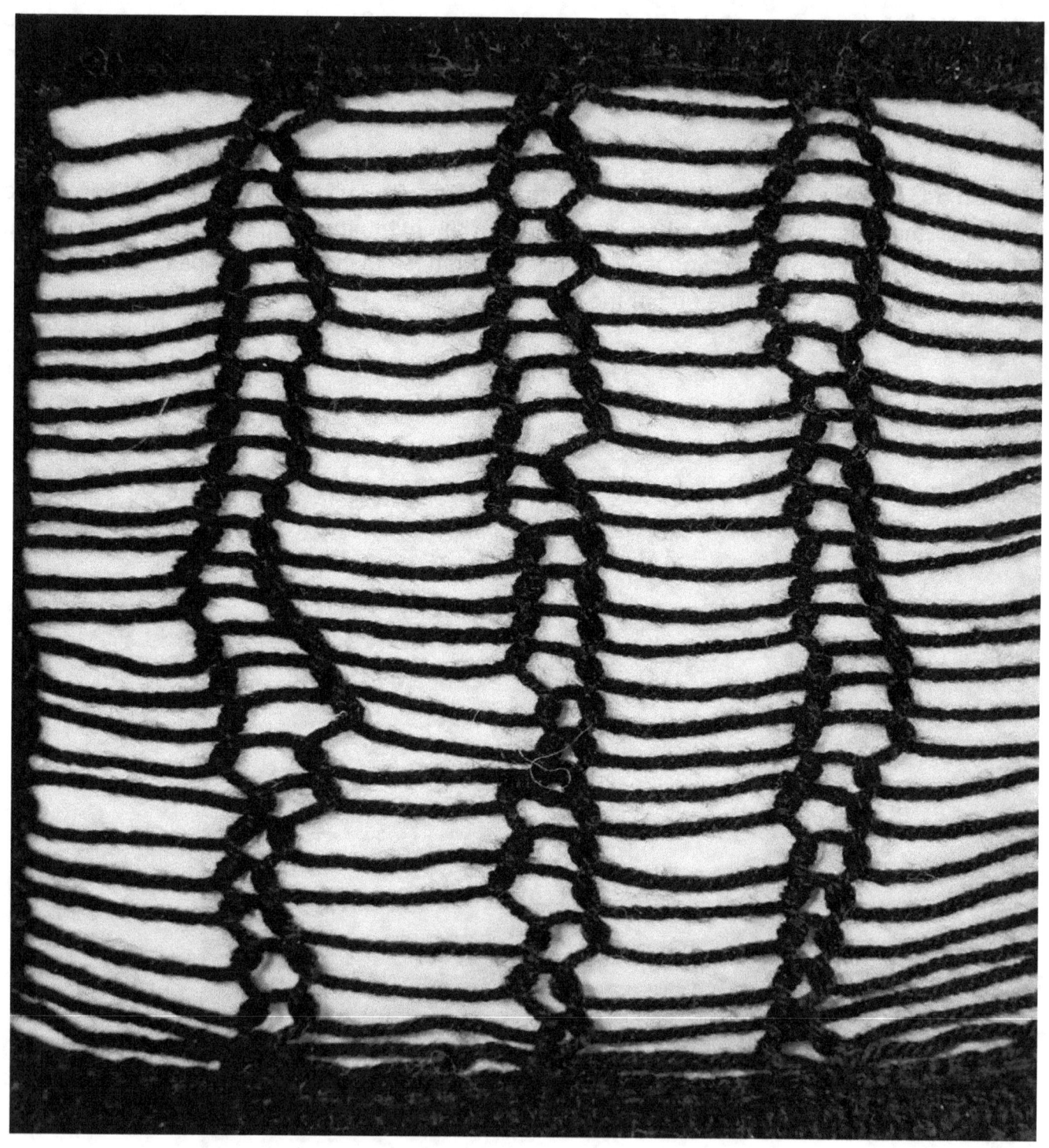

Cast on a multiple of 11, plus 1 for symmetry, and 2 edge stitches. **The edge stitches are not included in the description below and must be added. Slip the first edge stitch, purl the last one.**

**Knit through the back leg, purl as follows:** with the working yarn in front of the stitch, insert the right needle through the stitch from back to front, then move the working yarn under the right needle and pull it with the needle through the stitch. The purl stitch that is worked this way sets up the knit stitch to be knitted through the back leg.

**Note:** Knit a sample to determine the exact size of a future net, as it will increase approximately in half at the end of your work.

## Description:

**Bottom trim:**

**Row 1:** Knit all the stitches.

**Row 2:** Purl all the stitches.

**Row 3:** Knit all the stitches.

**Row 4:** Purl all the stitches.

**Row 5:** Bind off as follows: After the last row 4, turn your work over. Front Side: Slip all the stitches from the left needle to the right one (as a result, the working yarn is at the end of the right needle); turn your work over. Back Side: Slip 2 onto the right needle purlwise, insert the left needle through the 1$^{st}$ stitch, from left to right, and pass it over the 2$^{nd}$ one (now there is 1 stitch on the right needle), *slip 1 onto the right needle (now there are 2 stitches on the right needle), insert the left needle through the 1$^{st}$ stitch, from left to right, and pass it over the 2$^{nd}$ one (now there is 1 stitch on the right needle)* repeat from * to * until the end of the row. Leave the last stitch on the right needle and turn your work over, to the Front Side.

**Net:**

**Row 1 (Front Side):** Now there is 1 stitch on the right-hand needle (the edge stitch of the previous row). Take the left-hand needle. **From left to right,** pick up the left edge stitch and then the next 1 stitch out of the chain of bound off stitches onto the left-hand needle, inserting the left-hand needle from back to front; now there are 2 stitches on the left-hand needle; pick up every 11$^{th}$ stitch—from back to front— onto the left-hand needle until the right edge stitch (now all the stitches are on the left-hand needle and the right edge stitch is on the right-hand needle); work this row as follows: *knit 1, yarn over forward (i.e., from yourself) 3 times* repeat from * to * until the end of the row before the edge stitch, knit 1.

**Row 2:** *Purl 1, purl 1 (yarn over of the previous row), knit 1 (yarn over the previous row), purl 1 (yarn over of

the previous row* repeat from * to * until the end of the row before the edge stitch, purl the last 1.

**Row 3:** Knit all the stitches.

**Row 4:** Purl all the stitches.

**Repeat rows 3-4** until the desired length. After the last row 4, turn your work over.

**The last row (Front Side):** Take an extra needle, instead of the right-hand one. Slip the first 2 stitches of the net—the right edge stitch and the 1st stitch—onto the extra needle. *Slip the next 3 stitches off the left-hand needle (3 former yarn overs of the 1st row) and leave them as they are, then pick up the next 1 stitch onto the extra needle* repeat from * to * until the edge stitch, then slip the edge stitch onto the extra needle. Now the working yarn is at the end of the row. Turn your work over, to the Back Side. Take another extra needle. Back Side: Slip all the stitches from the left-hand needle onto the right-hand one. Turn your work over, to the Front Side. **Leave the needle with the open stitches of the net as they are.**

**Note:** Knit the top trim separately as described below, then bind off the stitches of the net together with the corresponding stitches of the top trim, thus connecting the net with the top trim.

**Top trim:**

Cast on a multiple of 11, plus 1 for symmetry, and 2 edge stitches. Knit 4 rows as follows:

**Row 1:** Knit all the stitches.

**Row 2:** Purl all the stitches.

**Row 3:** Knit all the stitches.

**Row 4:** Purl all the stitches.

**Row 5:** Bind off after the last row 4 as follows: Turn your work over. Front Side: Slip all the stitches from the left needle to the right one (as a result, the working yarn is at the end of the row); turn your work over, to the Back Side.

Juxtapose the needle with the top trim and the needle with the net as follows: the needle with the net must be in front of the needle with the top trim by the knit side up; the needle with the top trim must be behind the needle with the net by the purl side up.

Bind off the stitches of the top trim on the purl side together with the corresponding stitches of the net on the knit side as follows: slip the edge stitch from the extra needle with the net onto the right needle, slip the edge stitch from the needle with the top trim onto the right needle (now there are 2 stitches on the right needle), then insert the left needle through the 1st stitch on the right needle, from left to right, and pass it over the 2nd one;

*now there is 1 stitch on the right needle, slip 1 purlwise from the extra needle with the net onto the right one (now there are 2 stitches on the right needle), slip 1 from the needle with the top trim onto the right needle (now there are 3 stitches on the right needle), insert the left needle through the first 2 stitches on the right needle, from left to right, and pass them over the 3rd one (now there is 1 stitch on the right needle);

bind off the next 10 stitches of the top trim as follows: slip 1 from the needle with the top trim onto the right needle (now there are 2 stitches on the right needle), insert the left needle through the 1st stitch on the right needle, from left to right, and pass it over the 2nd one, repeat 9 more times*

repeat from * to * until the last 2 stitches on the extra needle with the net (the last stitch and the edge stitch), the last 2 stitches on the left needle with the top trim (the last stitch and the edge stitch), and the last 1 stitch of the top trim on the right needle;

Slip 1 from the extra needle with the net onto the right needle (now there are 2 stitches on the right needle), then slip 1 stitch of the top trim from the left needle to the right one (now there are 3 stitches on the right needle), then insert the left needle through the first 2 stitches on the right needle, from left to right, and pass them over the 3rd one (now there is 1 stitch on the right needle), then slip the edge stitch of the top trim from the left needle to the right one (now there are 2 stitches on the right needle), then slip the edge stitch of the net onto the right needle (now there are 3 stitches on the right needle), insert the left needle through the first 2 stitches, from left to right, and pass them over the 3rd one.

**Now slide down—from top to bottom—all the stitches that were slipped off the left needle and left as they are in the last row of your work, thus forming a net.**

# Pattern 50

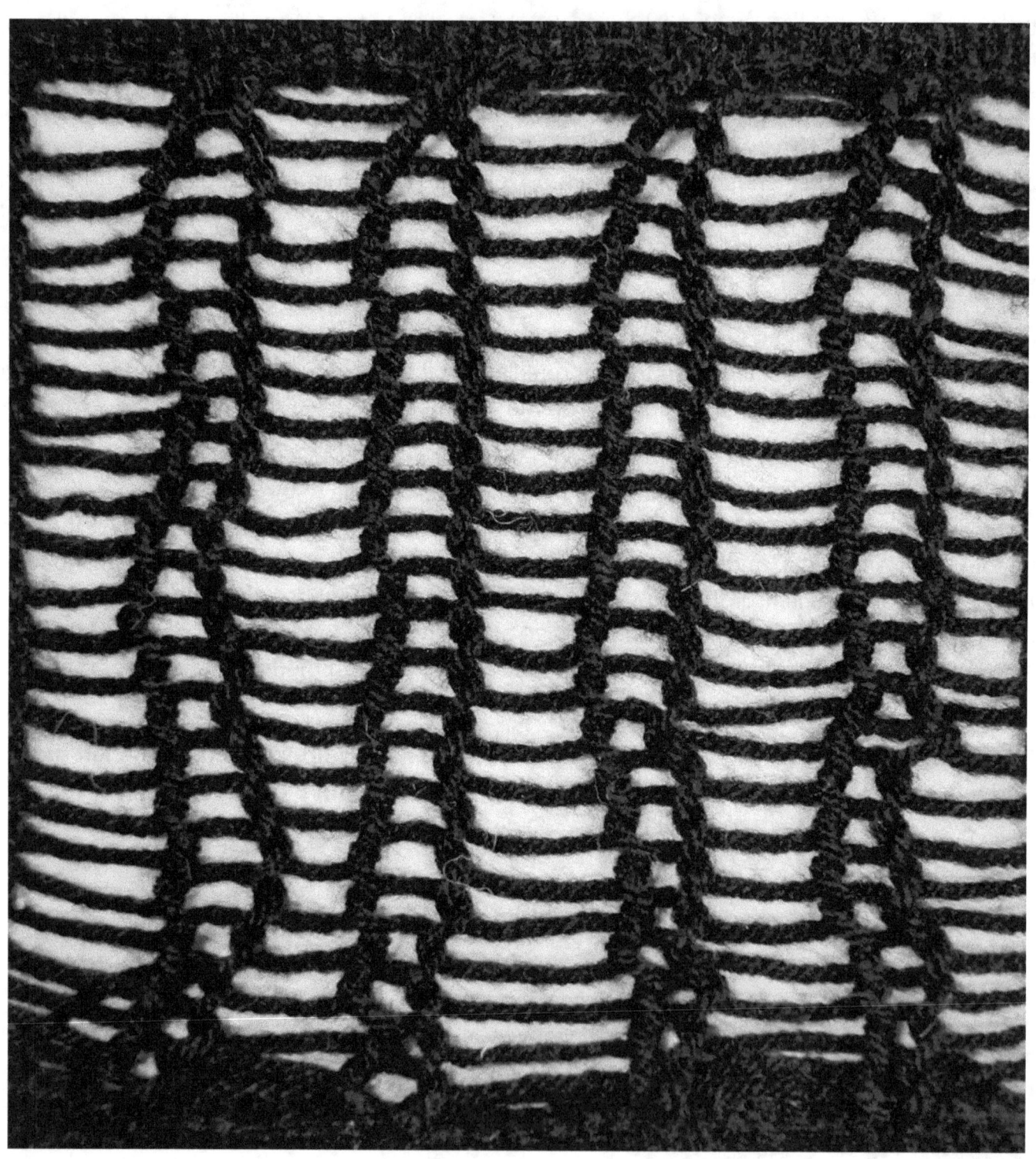

Cast on a multiple of 8, plus 1 for symmetry, and 2 edge stitches. **The edge stitches are not included in the description below and must be added. Slip the first edge stitch, purl the last one.**

**Knit through the back leg, purl as follows:** with the working yarn in front of the stitch, insert the right needle through the stitch from back to front, then move the working yarn under the right needle and pull it with the needle through the stitch. The purl stitch that is worked this way sets up the knit stitch to be knitted through the back leg.

**Note:** Knit a sample to determine the exact size of a future net, as it will increase approximately in half at the end of your work.

## Description:

**Bottom trim:**

**Row 1:** Knit all the stitches.

**Row 2:** Purl all the stitches.

**Row 3:** Knit all the stitches.

**Row 4:** Purl all the stitches.

**Row 5:** Bind off the trim as follows: After the last row 4, turn your work over. Front Side: slip all the stitches from the left needle to the right one (as a result, the working yarn is at the end of the row); turn your work over. Back Side: Slip 2 onto the right needle purlwise, insert the left needle through the 1$^{st}$ stitch, from left to right, and pass it over the 2$^{nd}$ one; *now there is 1 stitch on the right needle; slip one onto the right needle (now there are 2 stitches on the right needle), insert the left needle through the 1$^{st}$ stitch, from left to right, and pass it over the 2$^{nd}$ one* repeat from * to * until the end of the row. Leave the last stitch on the right needle and turn your work over to the Front Side.

**Net:**

**Row 1 (Front Side):** Now, there is 1 stitch on the right needle (the edge stitch of the previous row). Take the left-hand needle. **From left to right**, pick up the left edge stitch and then the next one stitch out of the chain of bound off stitches onto the left needle, inserting it from back to front (now there are 2 stitches on the left needle); pick up every 8$^{th}$ stitch onto the left needle, inserting it from back to front, until the right edge stitch; leave the right edge stitch on the right needle, then work this row as follows: *knit 1, yarn over forward (i.e., from yourself) 2 times* repeat from * to * until the end of the row before the edge stitch, knit 1.

**Row 2:** *Purl 1, purl 1 (yarn over of the previous row), knit 1 (yarn over the previous row), purl 1 (yarn over of the previous row* repeat from * to * until the last 2 at the end of the row, then purl 1, purl the edge stitch.

**Row 3:** Knit all the stitches.

**Row 4:** Purl all the stitches.

**Repeat rows 3-4** until the desired length.

**The last row (Front Side):** Take an extra needle, instead of the right-hand one. Slip the first 2 stitches of the net—the edge stitch and the $1^{st}$ stitch—onto the extra needle; *slip the next 2 stitches off the left needle (2 former yarn overs of the $1^{st}$ row) and leave them as they are, then pick up the next 1 stitch onto the extra needle* repeat from * to * until the end of the row, slip the edge stitch onto the extra needle (now the working yarn is at the end of the row); turn your work over, to the Back Side. Take another extra needle. Back Side: Slip all the stitches from the left extra needle to the right one. Turn your work over to the Front side. **Leave this extra needle with the open stitches of the net as they are.**

**Note:** Knit the top trim separately as described below, then bind off the stitches of the net on the extra needle together with the corresponding stitches of the top trim, thus connecting the net with the top trim.

**Top trim:** Cast on a multiple of 8, plus 1 for symmetry, and 2 edge stitches. Knit 4 rows as follows:

**Row 1:** Knit all the stitches.

**Row 2:** Purl all the stitches.

**Row 3:** Knit all the stitches.

**Row 4:** Purl all the stitches.

**Row 5:** Bind off as follows: After the last row 4, turn your work over. Front Side: Slip all the stitches from the left needle to the right one (as a result, the working yarn is at the end of the right needle); turn your work over to the Back Side. Juxtapose the needle with the top trim and the extra needle with the net as follows: the extra needle with the net must be in front of the needle with the top trim by the knit side up; the needle with the top trim must be behind the extra needle with the net by the purl side up.

Bind off the stitches of the top trim (purl side) together with the corresponding stitches of the net (knit side) as follows: Slip the edge stitch from the extra needle with the net onto the right needle, slip the edge stitch from the needle with the top trim onto the right needle (now there are 2 stitches on the right needle), then insert the left needle through the $1^{st}$ stitch on the right needle, from left to right, and pass it over the $2^{nd}$ one;

*now there is 1 stitch on the right needle; slip the next 1 purlwise from the extra needle with the net onto the right one (now there are 2 stitches on the right needle), slip 1 from the needle with the top trim onto the right needle (now there are 3 stitches on the right needle), insert the left needle through the first 2 stitches on the right needle, from left to right, and pass them over the 3rd one (now there is 1 stitch on the right needle); bind off the next 7 stitches of the top trim as follows: slip 1 from the needle with the top trim onto the right needle (now there are 2 stitches on the right needle), insert the left needle through the 1st stitch on the right needle, from left to right, and pass it over the 2nd one, repeat 6 more times* repeat from * to * until the last 2 stitches on the extra needle with the net (the last stitch and the edge stitch), the last 2 stitches on the left needle with the top trim (the last stitch and the edge stitch), and the last 1 stitch of the top trim on the right needle;

Slip 1 from the extra needle with the net onto the right needle (now there are 2 stitches on the right needle), then slip 1 stitch of the top trim from the left needle to the right one (now there are 3 stitches on the right needle), then insert the left needle through the first 2 stitches on the right needle, from left to right, and pass them over the 3rd one (now there is 1 stitch on the right needle), then slip 1 (the edge stitch of the top trim) from the left needle to the right one (now there are 2 stitches on the right needle), then slip the edge stitch of the net onto the right needle (now there are 3 stitches on the right needle), insert the left needle through the first 2 stitches, from left to right, and pass them over the 3rd one.

**Now slide down—from top to bottom—all the stitches that were slipped off the left needle and left as they are in the last row of your work, thus forming a net.**

# About The Author

Internationally recognized hand knitwear designer Marina Molo has taught on various aspects of hand knitting over the past 30 years. In her book, **50 Shades of Stitches Vol. 4,** Marina Molo brings to life, in print, most popular knitting patterns, **Mesh Knitting Patterns**, for all those who want to explore designing their own knitwear.

Visit the author's online store for unique items with knit prints, which include tank tops, leggings, tote bags, iphone cases, passport holders, luggage tags, wrapping paper, ribbons, pattern folders & much more at https://www.zazzle.com/store/shades_of_stitches or scan QR:

Marina Molo is currently working on several new publishing projects with SCR Media Inc.

Sign up to be notified when the next release is available at **www.MarinaMolo.com**.

# What Do You Think of 50 Shades of Stitches?

Thank you for purchasing this book, **50 Shades of Stitches Volume 4**

I hope that it adds value and quality to your everyday life.

If you like this book, I'd like to hear from you and hope that you could take some time to post a review on Amazon. Your feedback and support will help the author to improve her writing craft for future projects and make this book better. Just type this link into your web browser Getbook.at/Vol4 or scan code below:

I want you, the reader, to know that your review is very important and so, if you'd like to leave a review, all you have to do is copy into your web browser **Getbook.at/Vol4**.

I wish you all the best in your future success!

www.ingramcontent.com/pod-product-compliance
Lightning Source LLC
Chambersburg PA
CBHW081450070526
44586CB00019B/2288